**Children
of the
Howling Desert**

By
B Foshée

Copyright © 2014 by B Foshée
All rights reserved. No part of this book may be reproduced, scanned, or distributed in any printed or electronic form without permission.
First Edition: April 2014
Printed in the United States of America
ISBN: 978-162030969-8

For Jewel

Introduction

"Truth is stranger than fiction, but it is because Fiction is obliged to stick to possibilities; Truth isn't." -- Mark Twain

Domestic violence is intentional violence inflicted against a family member. The purpose of domestic or family violence is to dominate and control the victim. Domestic violence is not a single isolated act, but a pattern of physical, psychic, emotional, and psychological abuse that occurs systematically over a period of time. Families that experience domestic violence keep to themselves and are commonly socially isolated. Social isolation prevents the victims in these families from reaching out for help because of shame, fear, and psychological suppression with rules established by the abuser. Abusers maintain power and control by blaming the victim/s for the abuse. In these families, the abuser is all-powerful and omnipotent, and the victim/s powerless. As the abuse continues in private, away from the prying eyes of the public, domestic violence is very often a family dynamic passed on from generation to generation.

According to a 2013 study conducted by the U.S. Department of Justice, Bureau of Justice Statistics, 25% of women in the United States have experienced domestic violence. There are an estimated 960,000 incidences of domestic violence yearly. 85% of domestic violence victims are women and 15% are male. Only 25% of these incidences are reported to authorities. The highest predictor for generational transmission of domestic violence is a child's exposure to the father abusing the mother. This book is about growing up amongst generational violence, and the mental illness that is either a result or the reason.

You might ask why I wrote this book, and why now? I'll answer that. In lieu of current news events, families continue to live with the specter of violence hanging over their every day lives. The pattern continues.

It was time for me to stop being a coward, to stop being a part of the cover up. It was time for me to tell the truth, time for me to let you in on the reality of the family dynamic of violence. We, as a society, have not yet come to terms with the devastation some families are left with in the wake of violence in the home. I hear it all the time.

"My dad beat my mom, and it didn't effect me!--Well, my parents whupped me, and I turned out all right.--You can't intrfere with my right to discipline my child.--My parents slapped me, and I turned out all right. What's wrong with it?"

In the 21st century, how is it that we are still having this debate? If you hit a stranger on the street, that stranger has the right to prosecute you! Why would it be okay to hit loved ones? Can we all let go of the notion that violence in the home is an acceptable practice, that it is a private affair?

One

"It'll be different this time."

That's what Momma said when she had the inclination to take him back.

"Your Poppa's found God and he promised to do better. Everything's going to be all right now."

That's what she believed. But in order for everything to be all right, she and Poppa would have to be two entirely different people. And that was highly unlikely. They were intertwined in the dance of violence. And as long as they were, nothing would ever be all right; nothing would ever change.

A year later, they face each other across the kitchen table. Sitting between them is a pack of cigarettes, an ashtray filled with stubbed out butts, and a coffee pot. Gazing at him all moon-eyed and loving, she takes a sip of coffee leaving a half moon of red lipstick perched on the rim of the mug. She is eight months pregnant. Marveling at the way they've come together for this auspicious occasion while trying not to be too conspicuous, I eavesdrop on the conversation.

"We need to keep the tradition going," he announces with an air of irritation. "If you want to keep the initials ARF, we're going to have to come up with a good middle name."

That's ARF, the sound a dog makes—first name beginning with an A; the middle an R; the last an F for Foushée; the family surname. I guess the tradition hadn't been invented when I was born because my first name begins with a B, but everyone calls me by my middle name,

Leanne. The tradition must have started when my brother Aaron was born. He's Aaron Ray. Next came Jewel Avery, then Socorro Olivia.

They spend some time sifting through the possibilities, bantering name combinations back and forth . . . Alison Ruby . . . Alan Robert . . . Alice Rachel . . . Andrew Ryan . . . Ariel Rhea. After an hour, he impatiently throws his hands in the air.

"Well, if it's a boy, we'll name him after me, and a girl for you." Momma nods assent.

When the baby is born, they name her Anna Phoebe.

Two

Rules, rules, and more rules. No privacy allowed. The door to the room must be kept open at all times. You'd better look busy every waking moment. No lying on the bed during the day. Even when he wasn't around, the rules applied because there was no telling when he'd appear, and there was no crime worse than getting caught napping. According to my father, Ruben, I faked migraines to garner his sympathies. But that simply wasn't true because the only emotions pouring from him toward me were anger and hatred; neither of which could be misconstrued as empathy, or sympathy. Whether he believed it or not, the headaches were real, sometimes so bad that blurry vision, nausea, light sensitivity, and dizziness were the result. At the time, I didn't know migraines existed . . . just thought maybe, a brain tumor would eventually and mercifully put me out of my misery.

Leaning against the metal bed frame, I sat cross-legged on the floor cautiously facing the door. Grabbing the thickest from a neatly piled stack of books on the nightstand, I listen for footsteps. Nothing. Furtively tweezing a dog-eared notebook from its hiding place between the mattress and box springs, I lay it across the open book and lovingly rifle through the fluffy, soft as cotton pages until finding the one titled Freedom Plan. The sixteen year old girl who'd written the list almost three years ago is not the same one reading it now. Only months from turning nineteen, she is resolute and world-weary. Pretending to study for an exam already taken a week ago, with pencil in hand, I tick off each item for the thousandth time.

    1. Get a job. Check.

    2. Save money. Check.

    3. Try out for Up With Folks. Erased. Smudged. Apply for flight attendant jobs—major airlines listed. Erased. Smudged as well. Apply to the University of Kansas. Check.

    4. When accepted, go to Lawrence. Get a job. Check.

    5. Rent an apartment. Check.

    6. Move.

With everything completed but the move, breaking the news to Momma and Ruben is next. Pacing past the doorway, trying to act as though she doesn't want to interrupt, Momma leans in, pauses and then walks away. She's back fifteen minutes later, and she's agitated in a way that says she's out of cigarettes, or coffee, or both, and needs me to go to the store. And, as usual, she'll expect me to pay for them since she almost never has any money. I put her off and concentrate on making another list—THINGS I NEED FOR MY NEW APARTMENT. Carefully weighing the importance of each item, and whether it will be needed now or later, takes up another thirty minutes. The next time she comes back I acknowledge her presence.

"Momma, is something wrong?"

"Do you have any money," she blurts with controlled irritability.

"Yes."

"Can you go to the store and get a carton of cigarettes for me? And I'm almost out of coffee, too."

Viceroy 100's and Folgers drip grind; I know the two by heart. Minutes later, I lay the cigarettes in front of her on the kitchen table and proceed to pour water into the coffeemaker. I open the can I've just bought and scoop dark grains into the basket to start a fresh pot. Waiting for the coffee to brew while wistfully staring out the window into the evening darkness, my eyes shift perspective to the reflection in the window. Momma sits staring down at her hands, frowning—a plume of smoke wafting from her lips in a long, slow exhalation. Flavoring hers with lots of sugar and cream just the way she likes, I place a mug on the placemat in front of her. Cupping my hands around mine as though they need warming (it's unseasonably warm, about 85 degrees), I slide into the chair directly across from her.

"Momma, I need to tell you something," I say softly. Her head slowly tilts my way. I wait for her eyes to meet mine before continuing.

"I have a job and an apartment, and I'm moving to Lawrence in two days."

Cheerless eyes bore through my soul as the dawning of what I've said slowly comes to light on her face in a battle of changing expressions--a half smile to a frown of disappointment.

"You're selfish, just like your father," she spits.

"Momma, if Poppa is so selfish, why are you still with him? And if I'm just like him, you should be happy to see me go!"

With shaky hands, she lights another cigarette from the butt of the last, and takes a long, deep drag. I light one, too.

"When did you do all of this?"

"I took a day off work last week."

In order to keep my intentions unknown before leaving that morning, I'd left a couple packs on the table so she wouldn't need to call me at work.

"Why didn't you tell me you were thinking about leaving?"

"Because you would've tried to stop me."

"What about your sisters and brother? What will they do? I can't believe you're leaving me alone with him!"

And there it is; the manipulation that's kept me here this long. Over the last year I've avoided engaging with her or Ruben as much as possible. I've kept my head down pretending to be okay with the small violent world in their house. My days start early, long before she gets up, and end late at night, usually long after they've gone to bed. Most of the time, I'm either at work, or Community College, or dropping off one of my sisters somewhere, or running errands for them, or sitting in my car in the mall parking lot.

I work two part time jobs, one in retail, the second for a 24-hour answering service. That 24-hour thing is the perfect excuse not to be around. When coworkers want to be home with their families, I jump at the chance to work vacant shifts—graveyards, holidays, weekends. My employers sometimes ask if I'd like a day off but, politely, I decline. As a result of my industriousness, I've managed to save enough money to rent an apartment, and put away a rainy day fund. It's been difficult because they borrow money from me all the time. So, I learned to lie when he asks how much I make, or how much money I have in the bank. Otherwise, they would find some reason take it all. Sometimes he confronts me about how I should save more money than I do, and how I am irresponsible for not having done so. I keep my bankbook hidden under the rubber mat in the trunk of my car, under the jack.

"Momma, I can't save you anymore. It's not fair for you to expect me to!"

"And people in hell want ice water! Whoever said life was fair?" she retorts angrily.

"But nothing will change unless you do something about it. I hate him, and I hate living here, so I'm changing it!"

Trying to talk sense into her is like walking a tightrope because she has the tendency to lash out in anger when she doesn't get her way. Usually I tread lightly, but this time I'm prepared to sleep in my car if I have to. What have I got to lose?

"Aren't you afraid?" she asks after a long, terse silence.

"Couldn't be any worse than living here," I answer dispassionately. "Momma, you don't have to live like this. Now that Arianne's in school, you could get a job."

"But he doesn't want me to work."

"Then what are you going to do? Why not use your education to be independent?"

"But I don't want to teach anymore."

"You're not going to have more kids, are you?"

"Oh, no! I'm too old for that. Why would you ask a question like that? How dare you!"

Why? How dare I? Because of their penchant for reproductive dishonesty, that's why. Because it's part of the unspoken deal they've made. Because her life's work has been having kids—that's why! She gets pregnant. They stay together. She's only thirty eight. I drop the subject.

Ruben goes through his repertoire of manipulations searching for one that will work because that's what he does.

"It's only May. School doesn't start until September. What's your rush? And what about your sisters and brother? Are you really going to leave them behind?"

You'll notice both of them ask, "What about your sisters and brother," as if I were the parent. No mention is made of the violence, or the fear of violence and brutality that is sure to come my way if I stay. It's all about control, narcissistic control—sociopathic—manipulative control. One of the remaining siblings, more than likely a girl, will be shuffled into the vacuum left by my departure. Ruben and Momma will tell her it's because I abandoned them, and she and the others will come to resent me for it. I see it coming. Every time Momma says, "Why can't you be more like Leanne," I cringe. Why more like me? Why throw me up in their faces? The thought makes me boiling mad. But no one is allowed anger in this family, except him. So, to keep the bitterness out of my voice, I say in as measured a tone as I can muster, "It's time for me to go."

"Well, you better not take any of my shit out of this house!" That's what he said . . . not, "Take care of yourself"—or— "I'm proud of you"—or—"I'll miss you."

The moment of departure plays out in my head a million times. Hug my brother and sisters. Check. Walk out the door, get in my car and drive off into the sunset. Reality doesn't play out the same as I imagined. As usual, they put on a show for the rest of the world by following in their car for the thirty minute drive from Kansas City, Kansas to Lawrence, Kansas.

After picking up the keys from the rental office, I busy myself unloading the car, scrubbing the kitchen and bathroom, hanging clothes in the closet, and unfurling bedding to make a pallet on the floor since I didn't have a bed yet. I do all this while they sit in dumbfounded silence invading my space. They're probably thinking things like, "What am I going to do now?"—Or — "Who's going to look out for the kids?"—Or— "What about me?"

Locking the door behind them, I take a long slow exhalation of relief, check the locks on the windows, take a thirty minute shower for the first time ever, change into sweats, brush my teeth, turn on the TV, and slip between the covers. How wonderful it is that I've escaped. It's over! It's finally over!

Lawrence is laid back and peaceful in summer because most students won't arrive until September. I make myself at home with a routine of the mundane. I like the mundane. I go to work. I come home. I eat. I clean. I do laundry at the complex's laundromat. That's where I meet Amanda my first week. We make conversation, joke and laugh as if we've known each other forever. While sitting side-by-side atop the washers, she asks, "Hey, what's your story any way? How come you're here so early?"

"Oh, I just figured it was time for me to be on my own."

"You too, huh? Me, I couldn't get away from my alcoholic stepfather fast enough. Got tired of getting my ass kicked when he went on his benders, and then, listening to my mother's excuses for him. I haven't been back there in a year, and I don't intend to ever go back."

I'm in awe of her ability to be an open book because talking about my story is difficult. I think it. It swirls in my head, but my mouth can't speak it, like my teeth are glued together whenever the subject comes up. Regardless, we become fast friends, and partners in fun, made even more convenient by the fact that we live just a couple doors down from each other. Together we hit up the Opera House every Friday and Saturday night to listen to music, drink beer, meet people, dance and party, and explore newfound freedoms, just as I had always dreamed.

Current domestic violence literature and research suggests that escaping from the abuser is more likely to be successful when there is a plan in place. This plan should include caching items needed for a new life--birth certificates, money and credit cards, medications, children's school and immunization records, identification, important phone numbers, keys, clothing, etc.

Three

The air crackles dry with the kind of static electricity that portends a coming storm. During hot Southwestern summers, temperatures hover around the century mark for weeks on end. On a blistering day in July, Aaron and I take an egg from Momma's refrigerator and fry it on the sidewalk. In five minutes a big yellow eye, surrounded by a rubbery white sclera, stares at us from the middle of one of the concrete slabs in front of our house. The absurdity strikes us as funny. We can't stop giggling.

El Paso is a place of drifting sand, rocky outcrops, scrub-brush, and the heat-drenched asphalt of burgeoning suburban development. We live in a subdivision built to accommodate the influx of military families stationed at Fort Bliss, and Biggs Air Base. Despite the desert backdrop, lush squares of meticulously manicured blue-green Bermuda grass punctuates the front lawn of each matchbox house . . . all high and tight, nice and tidy, and squared away the military way.

Sirens wail. We Duck and Cover at school—jump under our kiddie desks, ball up tight, chins tucked, heads down, thumbs plugging the ears, the remaining eight fingers over the eyes. Every time I squat under one of them, it reminds me of my feeble attempts to protect my back from the lash of the belt. There is no escape.

The Base movie theater plays Westerns or war flicks. Instead of previews, violent cartoons and a propaganda newsreel run before the main feature. Typically the newsreel is about gas-masked men swaggering out of a cloud of radiation dust. Because I really want to know, I ask Mrs. Hulse, my third grade teacher.

"How can we survive a nuclear holocaust by Ducking and Covering?"

Every eye in the class stares straight at me with that look. You know the one. The disdainful one that says, "You idiot!" They believe. Me—I'm not so convinced. Mrs. H. seems taken aback, as though this was the first time she'd ever considered the prospect. Cocking her head, she answers, "I'm not sure. It might, but no one knows for sure."

It probably won't, but she had to keep the parents of her charges from coming down on her for telling the truth. Temperatures drop a few degrees with the setting sun. When everyone's gone to bed, Aaron and I sneak out of the house to follow moonlight for a half-mile above the subdivision. At the foot of the mountain, we perch on the biggest boulder in the cairn to listen to the wind hiss between stony crevices. Sound carries differently here; it bounces from cactus to scrub brush, skips along the rubble field, glances off canyon walls and back again. Giant saguaros stand sentry in the distance, middle fingers pointed toward the night sky. Among them, the coyotes sing. We answer, echoing long high-pitched notes in unison. Ah wooooo, ah wooo, woooo! Transported on the breeze, our plaintive songs intertwine and reverberate off canyon walls. Neighborhood dogs join the cacophony— back and forth, back and forth we chorus, two of the desert's creatures, calling, and singing, and howling just like the others. The desert howls. We howl. Abruptly, we quiet and, one by one, so do the others until nothing's left but eerie calm and the hiss of windy snakes.

"He hates us," he pronounces at long last.

"Yeah, I guess you're right Aaron."

Shame, overwhelming shame.

We sit gazing into the darkness until the horizon glows, until hearing the guttural growls of garbage trucks, starting and stopping, filling cavernous metallic guts with the detritus of life in the subdivision. Without a word, we scramble down and run full out all the way back to the house, arriving just before the rest of the world awakens. He is twelve and I am fourteen.

I don't exactly know when I knew, but it was somewhere around the age of two. They brought him home from the hospital just nine days before my second birthday, and as I peered through the bars of the crib at the sleeping baby wrapped in blue, I knew.

Four

"Leanne, you're as phony as a thirteen dollar bill. Get your goddamned head out the clouds."

Ruben said the goddamned as though it were two separate, well-defined words, short pause between the god and the damned.

"You don't have what it takes to survive outside this family," he continues.

The theme of this rant is about how, at fifteen, I am not grounded in reality, and how I am stupid, useless, and aimless. Ironic that he says these things, especially when he expects me; no, assumes that my siblings, his children with Momma are my responsibility. When they do something wrong, it is not Momma he berates; it is me. He is right about one thing though; with my head in the clouds, I dreamt of nothing but the day I could legally walk away.

Saturday, August 16, 2008

CHP officer Hernandez recovers a khaki backpack, a trash bag filled with human waste, and a handful of loose-leaf notebook papers. Riffling through the tattered wallet in the decedent's back pocket, he discovers a California ID, fifteen dollars, and some VA papers—all of it, according to the ID, belonging to one Aaron Ray Foushez. The photo matches, but before making an official notification to the family, he'll run the prints through AFIS just to be sure. The backpack yields an array of flotsam; a pen, a pencil, a dog-eared notebook filled with drawings and disjointed writings in a childlike scrawl, a match book, a mailbox key, and a Yellow Pages phonebook, the pages of which, were likely used as toilet paper; all of it presumed to belong to the man laying lifeless under the yellow tarpaulin. Time of death: 12:15am.

He was hit by a commuter bus while crossing an East Los Angeles freeway, and died under what might be considered odd circumstances. Although the official cause of death was determined a pedestrian/vehicle collision, I believed—No! —I *knew* it was suicide. He'd finally done what he'd talked about for the last fifteen years. Other circumstances led me to this conclusion as well. For one, he'd been homeless for some time, and two, his death came nineteen days before his fiftieth birthday. When we were kids, he often said, "I'm not going to live to be very old." When asked what he considered old, he replied, "Fifty. Fifty years is too long."

As children, we'd been inseparable and managed to stay close until our mid thirties; until his symptoms became so acute I couldn't break through the scar tissue. In those last years, he was enigmatic, elusive and out of touch, cycling through paranoia and depression, PTSD flashbacks, and a chemical imbalance. And although military doctors had diagnosed him with schizophrenia, it is entirely possible he was misdiagnosed. Historically, the military doesn't have the best track record for dealing with mental illness among its troops and, since I knew his back story, I came to believe that Aaron actually suffered from a cocktail of undiagnosed, and untreated mental illnesses that he'd been self-medicating since the age of fourteen. Doctors had difficulty finding the right drug therapy and their inability to treat him was made more complex because he was combative and uncooperative, taking his meds sporadically, if at all. To top it off, because of how we grew up, he had major trust issues. Trusting a doctor, therapist, psychiatrist, or family member just wasn't going to happen. And I have to admit that when Momma first told me of his diagnosis, I didn't believe it because I didn't trust her.

During more lucid moments, he surfaced in my life for short, fragmental snippets of time through cryptic phone calls. Sometimes those lucid moments lasted six months, sometimes ten days, sometimes a year. Before the lucidity vanished, I'd try to get an address, or some clue as to his whereabouts. But as quickly as he appeared, he disappeared without any word. Poof, gone—phone disconnected—no forwarding address—lost—trapped inside the illness. I understood why he couldn't trust, and why he disappeared like that because I too disappeared from the family nearly thirty years prior and surfaced only when strong enough to deal with the ghosts of the past. I wanted my brother back, but which one would he be—the mischievous, fun-loving kid from childhood, or the secretive stranger I didn't know in adulthood?

According to Afifi, et al., (2009), some common consequences associated with child abuse and neglect are persisting mental health problems, personality disorders, dissociative disorders, psychosis, and post-traumatic stress. Additionally, abuse and neglect in early childhood is connected to the incidence of homelessness in adulthood (Lamont 2010). A study by Herman, Susser, Struening, and Link (1997) revealed that adults who experienced physical or sexual abuse during childhood were 26 times more at risk of homelessness in adulthood than those who had not.

Five

The gauntlet of airport concessionaires is no different than midway hawkers at a State fair. Having been buckled inside a flying tube for more than five hours, my immediate need is not food, gum, t-shirts, or magazines. Carry-on in tow, I ride the escalator to street level and speed walk past baggage claim . . . straight for fresh air. Automatic doors shush open releasing a blast of disappointment. Dallas in August is brutally hot and humid. Gauzy heat waves murmur low and heavy over the asphalt. Cars glide through the diaphanously muggy air in slow motion. Trapped inside the haze is the pungency of freshly laid tar and exhaust fumes. The time/temperature clock reads 11:01am, 101 degrees farenheit. Time inches along as my clothes suck warm moisture from the air. It sounds like someone shaking a paper wasps nest—the buzzing louder and angrier at each passing second. I feel like crawling out of my skin. I want it to be two days into the future. I don't want to be here because from the time I step into their world, I am acutely aware of the burning fuse. I'd been here in the beginning of June. To say, two visits in the same year is a rarity would be the truth because in thirty years I've been here maybe six times, and half of those were for crisis's. The first happened when my son, Omar was almost two. Allya, the youngest, drowned in a hot tub and was put on life support. Thankfully, she recovered in a matter of days and I quickly returned home.

The second came in 2008. Momma fell ill. Thinking it might be the last time I'd get to see her alive, I brought an eleven year old Omar with me. Against all odds, she improved, and we promptly returned home after four days.

The phone rang again in late-summer of the same year. Seconds ticked by and turned into minutes. Minutes stretched to eternity. I don't remember the rest of the conversation, if there was any, or hanging up, if I did. What I do remember is integrating with my body after an hour of stumbling around the house like a gut-shot zombie. The bad news requires another trip, one that I dread. The chaos is waiting to erupt because that's the resting state of the family in crisis.

The last time I visited just to visit, I still thought that one day we would all eventually have a great kumbaya, but that turned out to be a mistake. Before I arrived, Arianne announced her pregnancy to the family. Exciting changes seemed to be happening in her life; meeting Tom, falling in love, getting married. But those positive life events were sullied in an atmosphere of condemnation, resentment, anger, and contempt. And I landed smack dab in the middle of it. Momma didn't approve of Tom and, therefore, didn't support their marriage. Divisions among the factions were virulent. And to make matters worse, Momma's enlisted Socorro and Anna to gang up on the couple and sling mud as well. Congratulations should be in order, but everyone is bent on carrying out Momma's agenda because, for a short time, they will be on her good side. Our mother pits us against each other because she herself grew up in a chaotic household, married into a chaotic household and now recreates chaos as a normal response to life's pressures. The irony is not lost on me. Another lifetime ago, before understanding that things weren't likely to change no matter how long I stayed away, I desperately wanted to be a part of the family in a way that made sense.

Shortly after meeting my future life partner, I brought him along to Thanksgiving dinner at Momma's. He is beautiful, charming, well educated, and obviously madly in-love with me, and it is obvious I'm madly for him. Everyone seems to like him, except Ruben, who shows his disapproval by spending the day heaving up steaming piles of socially inept verbal emesis in a non-stop interrogatory. At the apex of nastiness, he asks Javier the magic question.

"What are you in school for?"

"Well sir, I'm working on my Ph.D. in psychology."

This nonchalant revelation shuts him down cold. His mouth moves, but no more venom spews forth. As he struggles to recover, everyone is witness to his discomfort.

"Well, I guess you're sitting here analyzing me right now then, aren't you, young fella?" he accuses loudly while simultaneously thumping his index finger on the table for emphasis.

Unflustered by the obvious animosity, Javier replies, "No sir, I'm here to meet my future in-laws."

Kaboom! Dead silence. Stares. Percolating lava bubbles from the depths. It's time to exit.

"He ain't shit. He's lyin' to you! He ain't gonna be no goddamned psychologist! Who the hell does he think he is insulting me like that in front of my own damn family? I survived the jungles of Vietnam . . . you know what that means, don't you . . . I deserve respect . . . I don't like him! Don't bring him around here no more, or don't you bother coming back!"

"Okay," I respond noncommittally.

"Okay, what," he asks with a sneer curling his upper lip.

Since he hasn't laid eyes on me in two years, I'm amazed he thinks anything that comes out of his mouth has any relevance. We don't have that kind of relationship. No point arguing with crazy. Javier and I get in the car and head home.

"What was all that about? Did I say something to offend him?"

"No, not at all! Now you know why I don't like being around my family, and why I don't have plans to come back any time soon. I've spent my life learning how not to be like them." The week had been filled with positive things like fun holiday parties and get-togethers, and my new love—until now.

"He was so disrespectful to everyone, especially to your mom. Is it always like that?"

I get it. Why shouldn't he ask? He needs to know what he's up against.

"That's why Aaron went MIA. He didn't want to be assaulted and demoralized."

"Why does your mom invite him?"

"Beats me. I specifically asked if he was going to be there. She said he hadn't been invited, but that was a technicality. If he happened to show up though, he was welcome to come in and disrupt the get-together. They've been divorced for five years by now, yet she's still unable to break the habit. The part I hate is how she makes excuses for why he is the way he is, and why we should put up with it. She denies it, but I think she wants him back. Invited, or not, all you did was answer a question. The reason he doesn't like you is he thinks you can see through his façade, and he's deathly afraid of being psychoanalyzed, deathly afraid of someone figuring out just how sick he really is, how sick she really is.

When we were kids, she blamed Aaron and me for her inability to leave him.

I could never leave your father because you all wouldn't let me.

That's what she'd say.

I ask Momma if her reasons for stirring the hostility toward Arianne and Tom were valid.

"He's thirty two; she's twenty seven. He's European-American; we're African-American. They're gainfully employed—not asking anyone for anything. They seem happy together. What's the big deal?"

In my eyes, Arianne's marriage meant that Momma would have to get a j-o-b and Socorro and Anna simply became the distractions from the real issues. With a new baby on the way, Arianne's income will no longer be available to pay Momma's bills. I hate stepping inside the time warp . . . inside a pit of writhing, ill-tempered rattlers. Initially, I'd planned to stay four days, but two is all I can take. You just need to forgive. That's what people say. Well of course I do, but forgiving doesn't mean I have to play stupid.

Although the drive from Love Field is pleasant enough, I feel out of place. Along the way, an obligatory stop for greasy fried food—chicken, fries, okra, and hush puppies; not the best choices considering Momma's hospitalization two months earlier. Her speech is a little slurred, and she can't find the right words. From what I've been told, her blood pressure was so high by the time they got to the hospital that it was off the charts.

She's never taken care of herself, not even under the direst circumstances. From as far back as I can remember, she's subsisted on a steady diet of specialty food groups like two or three packs of cigarettes per day, combined with two pots of sugar soaked coffee.. And what little she does eat consists of high salt, high sugar TV dinners, breaded and fried anything or vegetables boiled to mush and seasoned with, you got it, more fat and salt! Though she vehemently denies it, depression, an eating disorder, and addiction have been her lifelong friends. And pregnancy provided no impetus to eat healthily for the baby's sake. In those days, the debate about the detrimental effects of tobacco was still raging. The cigarette company's propaganda machine was still winning the war of words in advertisement and historical addiction research.

Mostly, I remember her drinking coffee and nervously chain-smoking, lighting the next cigarette with the dying ember of the last—in one breath boasting about how not eating has kept her slim, and the next, complaining about losing a tooth after each baby was born. I suspect her blood pressure and heart problems are the results of dietary deficiencies and poor health habits that have caught up to her. However, there's no need to preach. No one can hear me, so I hope to be gone by the time the fuse burns down to the stick of dynamite it's attached to.

Around midnight I fall into a restless sleep. Surging all around me is a sea of shuffling grey souls with out-of-focus faces. I drive deeper into the throng, an irony that makes me smile. The sea of souls part to let me pass. It's the story of my life; against the grain, wrong way, misguided Leanne. That's me! An organ note so beautiful, sweet, and perfect is struck sending reverberations into the rafters. The note transports me into the troposphere on a jet stream of ebullience. I'm in a flying dream . . . something I haven't experienced for quite some time. The next note is the high-pitched scream of a baby in severe distress. It sends me crashing to Earth in a stomach churning, broken-winged, end over end free fall—down—down—down into the heaviness of my Earth body. I jolt awake, sweaty and breathless and disoriented.

A study conducted by Thornton (2014), found domestic violence to have deleterious effects on family dynamics and relationships, forcing divided loyalties, suspicion of motives, reduction in family communication, interference with collaboration in decision-making, and non-reliance on predictability within the family.

Six

    Shadows move. The sweltering house creaks. My eyes slowly adjust to the darkness. Coming into focus—a chest of drawers—clothes hanging in the closet—my bag on the chair—the scratchy wool blanket of fresh grief. I think about Aaron and silently weep. I remember now. Momma's house—the upstairs bedroom—air conditioning on just low enough to keep the downstairs comfortable. She's used to the heat, has no inkling how prickly it gets up here. A gummy yellowish-brown film covers every surface. The house has a fierce case of halitosis mixed with OPS (old people's smell). The carpet is fetid and matted. An overpowering stench of nicotine and stale cigarette smoke permeates every crevice.

    I slide my feet into my slippers, pull on my robe and pad downstairs to lower the thermostat. Passing her room, my eyes are drawn to an otherworldly glow. Bathed in the flickering light of the TV, she sits in a straight-backed chair—head rolled backward, mouth wide-open, left hand aloft, elbow on the armrest as though she were wide awake. The only giveaway she's still alive is loud, gravelly snoring. Thin threads of smoke curl away from the long, crooked ash of the cigarette scissored between her index and middle fingers. This is not the first time she's fallen asleep with a lit cigarette. The duvet and pillow on her bed are marked with caterpillar-like burns. The carpet under her chair is pocked with blackened burn holes. Once they realize I am staring at the burns, Arianne and Socorro attempt to assure me there's nothing to worry about because they'd made her promise to sit in the chair while smoking, which is almost every moment of her existence.

"But aren't you afraid she will set the house on fire and go up in flames with it?"

Things have deteriorated over the past ten years. Since retiring from teaching in a GED program for over fifteen years, she counts on Socorro, Arianne, or Anna to do everything she should be doing for herself—grocery shopping, banking, doctor's appointments, or even walking the short distance to the mailbox to get her own mail. Retirement was just the perfect excuse to relinquish control of her day-to-day life, which, I believe, is what she's always wanted, and part of the reason she stayed with Ruben all those years. He made the decisions, and good, bad, or indifferent, she went along. Treated as nothing more than chattel, a piece of property, an unwanted, unloved, disrespected, offending appendage, she was allowed no identity of her own; so much so, she even signed her name Mrs. R. P. Foushée.

"I don't have to do anything for myself," she brags wistfully. "Socorro takes care of everything."

Sometimes I ask if that's fair to Socorro.

"Oh, don't worry about that. Socorro wants to take care of her dear old mother."

With the exception of an occasional trip to the doctor, or to one of her daughters' homes for Sunday dinner, she is set upon the shelf like a knick-knack, and left to self-imposed isolation and imprisonment—left to slowly commit suicide. I pluck the butt from her fingers and impatiently stub it out in the ashtray on the TV stand. I want to shake her awake. I want to stomp and yell, "You didn't give a damn about me when I was a kid! At least, give a shit now for my child's sake! I didn't come here to be burned up in a house fire caused by you falling asleep with a lit cigarette!" Instead, I gently shake her shoulder until her head snaps off the back of the chair.

"Momma, why don't you go to bed?"

"I will honey," she mumbles as she lights another.

I say goodnight, and leave her sitting in front of some infomercial about miracle weight loss. Once upstairs, I look for ways to escape in an emergency, just in case flames consume the stairs. The windows are ornamental, not functional. I guess I could smash one and jump, probably breaking a leg or hip in the process. But at least I'd be able to return home to my family. I check on her throughout the night. Close to daybreak, I catch the ashtray smoldering, and run water over the embers, leaving behind a nasty brown mess in the kitchen sink before going back up the stairs. Lying awake, tossing and turning, missing my family, I count off the slow moving hours before my flight home. Having slept no more than an hour or two all night, I am absolutely exhausted by daybreak. When I come downstairs to make coffee, I find that she has slept in the chair all night, and that she is oblivious to my fears.

"Momma, when I smelled smoke last night, I found your ashtray smoldering. I was afraid you'd set the house on fire with me in it."

"Oh honey, you don't need to worry about that."

It's the same as when I was a kid. I look out for her, but she doesn't look out for me. It's like she's saying, "You don't matter." Everyone tells me to meet her where she is.

I think to myself, "If she wants to kill herself, but she's not allowed to my life for granted because I don't want to go with her!"

Seven

We mill around communing with family, some of whom I haven't seen in more than three decades, some I've never met; sisters, uncles, aunts, cousins, nieces, nephews. Momma occasionally moves from the sofa to limp heavily to the bathroom.

"I've been dreading this day. It's one of the worst of my life," she mutters with a faraway look. Wreathed in flowers on the counter, is a picture of him in dress uniform. Looking directly into the lens that day, his essence was captured when the shutter clicked. The eyes are alive. Under hooded lids, they follow my every move. Every time I look up, I catch him staring. Why this photo I wonder? He detested his military days. But I have no doubt it was chosen because it protects the lie. Momma's extended family doesn't really know anything about us. We grew up in isolation. And today, it is mostly her family in attendance because most of Ruben's people are gone. He has managed to survive three younger brothers, his mother and father, most of his cousins, uncles, and aunts and now, his only son.

From somewhere in the room, Socorro's mirthless cackles can be heard over the din—like there is some inside joke to which I am not privy. Not to be outdone, Ruben, the ever-consummate showman and center of attraction sniggers jovially like he's at a party. They take turns vying for attention . . . cackle, cackle, cackle . . . he, he, he . . . cackle, cackle, cackle . . . he, he, he . . . long, sharp nails dragging slowly down a dry chalkboard. It's too off the wall, too bizarre, too dramaturgic, too film noir. Maybe a different perspective will help. I give up my place on the sofa next to Momma and circulate the room, fake smiling, and engaging others in conversation. Beneath a calm exterior a caged animal looks for escape, anxious, panting, pacing, to and fro, to and fro. Cackle, cackle, cackle, he, he, he—slow, high-pitched scraping that sets my teeth on edge.

At one point Socorro comes over to tell me how she completed all five stages of grief and loss yesterday during her morning run. Caught off-guard, I say something like, "Oh, that's good."

Uncle Lonnie, Momma's brother, asks what happened.

"You live in California. Did you see how it happened?"

I open my mouth to speak.

"We don't really know what happened," she answers crisply right behind me. I almost jump out of my skin. She's somehow managed to get off the couch, hobble over, and speak up just in time to keep the secrets.

Jewel is the only one missing, and I know why. Third in birth order, and exactly 361 days younger than Aaron, Momma doesn't like Jewel. Never has, never will. She treats Jewel with disdain, disrespect, and hatred because, as irrational as it may sound, she blames Jewel for ruining her life. I'm not exactly sure why, but it could be that Momma was pregnant when they returned to the States after Germany. As the years passed, Momma's bad behavior toward Jewel escalated. She once told me how she'd seen Jewel in the airport with a group of her co-workers. Jewel said, "Hi Momma," but Momma gave her the cold shoulder right in front of her peers. I was baffled that she would do that to her own daughter, and then act as though it was a righteous thing to do. I can only imagine how humiliated and hurt Jewel must have felt!

But not only does Momma do hurtful, passive-aggressive things to Jewel, she bad-mouths her to Socorro, or anyone willing to listen. When we were kids, our mother enjoyed making fun of her own children with darker skin color, while encouraging the rest of us to gang up on them as well. Though quite brown-skinned herself, she had a thing about dark-skinned people, like she was somehow superior. I am ashamed when I think about how I participated, how I was a part of hurting my siblings. I just wanted her love and approval, but that is no excuse. Now, when she attempts to get me to side with her against Jewel, I abruptly break off the interaction.

"Momma, I believe parents are responsible for having good or bad relationships with their children. We're the ones who set up the patterns for success or failure. She didn't choose to be born!"

Jewel left that house in her late teens, as I did, and moved to Memphis where she worked as a flight attendant. She raised her children on her own. And, like me, her visits were infrequent and short and only on her terms. And since our visits never coincided, we had not seen each other for more than twenty five years by the time our brother died. The divide and conquer strategy our parents perpetuated worked. I didn't know or trust her and she didn't know or trust me. Now that I'v put it all together, I'm sure she didn't come to Aaron's funeral because she had no trust that she would be safe in the situation.

Abueg & Fairbank (1992), found strong evidence that early childhood abuse causes lifelong feelings of being in danger, hypervigilance, distrust, and avoidant behavior when the abused is confronted with the system in which the original abuse occurred either by situation, or through therapy.

Eight

In fifth grade Social Studies, with pencil in hand, I attempt to resolve a weighty problem. Let's see—how old will I be in the year 2000? Forty five. The question and answer made me think about people in my circle who'd made it—two grandmothers, aunts, uncles, teachers. I probably wasn't going to be one of them though . . . didn't feel invincible like most my age. I felt vulnerable and at risk, so much so that there was no doubt I'd end up gasping for breath after sucking in burning ash from the great explosion. And if that didn't get me, the Nuclear Winter would.

Kneeling beside the bed each night I prayed over steepled hands. Now I lay me down to sleep. I pray the Lord my soul to keep. If I should die before I wake, I pray the Lord my soul to take.

Before the Amen, one silent request, a simple wish, a child's naïve bargain, "Don't let anything happen to him Lord, but please make him go away." I said that prayer a thousand times before my 10th birthday. That was a thousand times before the first epiphany hit. Everything wasn't going to be all right, and God wasn't going to come to my rescue from on high as promised in Sunday school! His answer had always been existential indifference. Why hadn't I gotten that before now?

Grinding a groove in a routine as common as getting up in the morning, taking a shower, eating breakfast, and walking to and from school, being bullied was a normal part of life. At school, my tormentors clocked in as self-appointed, self-important intimidators, aggressors, and half-baked idiots. Why me, you might ask? Over the years, I've asked that same question. I radiated victim energy. I was tiny and made an easy target. I was pretty, something I didn't know or feel back then. I was one of a handful of African-American kids in the school. But even with all that, in comparison to what went on in our house, schoolyard bullies were the least of my worries because once I graduated, cretins like that would have no place in my life.

Momma often said, "You'll get through it. Just keep saying, get thee behind me, Satan."

What did Satan have to do with it? Was he going to ream me, or back me up? According to Momma's Good Book, Satan is the sole cause for all the evil in the world, and the evil badass who vexes the "you know what" out of God. If that were true, why would I challenge him to a duel? I had enough problems as it was, didn't need to invite more! While Satan's purpose is to lead souls to the dark side, in strict opposition, God's authorities, flesh and blood Christian soldiers guide lost souls to the right side. If I bedded down with the Christian side I'd have to walk genuflected to keep the knives out of my back because the people I found most worrisome were those professing to be hardened Christians. My encounters with them left me questioning whether they batted for team Jesus, or team Satan.

"People are complicated. Could be both . . . a lot of gray area there. The Bible says evil comes in all forms, but Sunday is the day all sins are forgiven because it's the Lord's Day."

Her explanations were one-dimensional and juvenile and required me to believe either Satan, or Christian Soldiers were somehow responsible for the bullying, which I did not. What about people being complicated? And what about all that gray area? And why does the Lord have only one day, and Satan six?

"You need to turn the other cheek. Forgiveness is the only thing they understand."

That statement was not about school bullies. It was a double entendre . . . subtext . . . code referring to the many faces of her husband . . . my biological father . . . the bully in our house. When I attempted a meaningful conversation with her about my difficulties, she took it as an opportunity to unload her problems in a rant that usually ended on a pejorative note.

"What do you have to complain about? You're just a kid. This should be the most carefree time of your life. Come talk to me when you're an adult," she'd declare with an edge of contempt. To which I thought; if this is the best time of my life, what do I have to look forward to?

Her modus operandi was to deflect my reality and then scapegoat Aaron, Jewel, or me when Ruben beat her up. She turned her mind off; turned off that nagging inner voice telling her something was wrong, the one telling her to turn tail and run like the wind. And the brand of forgiveness she espoused required lying in front of the same on-coming 18-wheeler again and again. And just like the bullies at school, neither she, nor Ruben were obligated to take any responsibility. The devil made him do it, and she was an innocent bystander. Her best advice was to warn me not to get into fights because fighting was unladylike! I guessed that getting beat up was?

"When I was in college, there were girls living in the same dorm who didn't like me. All you have to do is ignore them," she'd finish.

But those girls weren't pulling her hair, pushing her down, throwing things at her, or following her home in threatening mobs. Junior year, I finally got fed up. One of the bullies pushed me and I lost control. When I came to, I was straddling her chest, punching her face. Her nosed was bloody, and she was crying. She was bigger; I was wiry and physically stronger. Punishment consisted of a three-day suspension from school, and an ass kicking from Ruben for embarrassing him. Nothing like getting a beating from a bully for defending yourself against a bully.

"Well," she continued, "Kids and dogs don't remember anything from when they're little. Trust me. You'll forget all about this."

To which, I'd ask, "Since I'm not going to remember, why do I have to go to school?"

My parents attempted to make me feel stupid for seeing what they told me not to by articulating inane, down-home colloquial expressions, compelling little kernels of wisdom that were supposed to be relevant to the situation at hand. "You don't know your head from a hole in the ground," or "You don't know shit from shine-ola," or "Get your head out of your ass." And the piece de resistance: "The devil exists in a buttered biscuit!"

Maybe they didn't know the difference between shit and shine-ola but, in my mind, there was a very clear distinction; one is excrement, feces, crap, the body's solid waste discharged through the anus, if you want to get technical; and the other is for shining shoes. One smells like wax. The other smells like, well . . . you get the picture. Oh! And by the way, I would have to be an extraordinary contortionist to get my head in or out of my own ass. As far as the devil in the buttered biscuit, alas I'm stumped!

Nine

"You know she pulls her hair out by the root, don't you?"

"No, Momma. I didn't know that. If that's true, why do you think she does it?"

"How would I know what's in her mind? She's a drunk. That might have something to do with it."

"You and Jewel haven't had a conversation in two decades! How would you know what she does? Who told you that?"

The only person's flaws she points out are Jewel's—the one not living in proximity of the family, the one not engaged in the family system, the one she knows very little about, the one she has scape-goated all her life. And she attempts to gossip to the one who also lives far away, the one not engaged in the day-to-day workings of the family system, the one she honestly knows little about.

In all honesty, all of us, including me, have maladaptive strategies for dealing with life's stressors. Ruben slapped me around to break me of the habit of biting my fingernails until they bled, so I moved underground to bloodletting . . . build up to the edge of explosion . . . prick of relief . . . the feeling of one perfect moment . . . cutting. When life got stressful, which was most every day I lived in that house of horrors, I took a large sewing needle I kept hidden in my mattress and stuck it into my fingers to watch the bead of blood form. Sometimes when the pressure was extreme, one prick had no effect. I pushed the needle in one side and out the other like a piercing—two beads of blood, one for each hole. Letting blood deflated the pressure. The need to quit in my late twenties brought me to a psychiatrist who prescribed Prozac. My fingertips healed for the first time since I was thirteen. I confessed my experiences with the OCD and the PTSD I'd kept hidden since childhood, but she refused to believe it. I told her about the trichotillomania, and eating disorders that seem to run in our family, but she refused to believe that as well. So, I asked, "Why do you think we all do it?"

"For attention, I guess," she replied. "You do it for attention."

"Momma, growing up in violence is not supposed to be normal. Our family suffers from, at the very least, psychiatric and personality disorders. And, at the most, hereditary mental illness on both sides! I want to do better. I want to get better, so I need to acknowledge it."

"Oh, no. You're wrong. Not on my side. Your dad's people are the crazy ones."

Ten

While absentmindedly pushing the medicine cabinet closed, she reads and rereads the skull and crossbones warning on the back of the aspirin bottle. A sharp metallic snap brings her eyes level with the salt stained face of a stranger in the mirror. Little, dried, creek beds cross at her chin under swollen cheeks, a fat, bloody lip, puffy red eyes, and a drop of coagulating blood at the corner of the right nostril. She finds a washcloth, wets it, and gently wipes the face in the mirror. Nothing. No feeling. He stands in the doorway, playing the broken record over the same discordant notes.

"You know I love you, sugar pie. You know your Poppa loves you. Don't you," he whines.

On cue, without looking away from the face in the mirror, the swollen lips move to the expected answer, the expected lie. Disconnected, disembodied, with flat affect, "I know you do, Poppa."

"You know you can always come to me for anything," he continues.

"I know I can," I lie.

"If you're having trouble in school, don't hesitate to ask me."

The exchange is a choreographed dance of lies because asking him for anything is tantamount to holding a blood vial in front of an emotional vampire.

In eighth grade, for a sundry of reasons, math is a foreign language. I don't get it and the teacher isn't at all helpful. My mantra is: "But why? I don't understand. Why am I doing this?"

"Don't worry about the why. Just do it," comes the reply.

That answer didn't work the first time he'd given it, nor the 50th. I still don't get it! Up to this point, I've at least excelled in school, but now I am set adrift with no oars or life vest—frustrated and failing. The chaos is unmanageable. I am drowning and nobody sees it . . . certainly not my parents. They see nothing beyond their little games. Earlier that day, I begged Momma for help.

"I can't. You know I'm terrible at math. You'll have to ask your father."

This answer comes from the same woman who, years later, wrote college papers so Arianne could complete her bachelor's degree. They had a deal. Arianne worked, and Momma didn't have to as long as she made sure Arianne passed her classes.

"But he'll beat me," I protest.

"No. Your father would never do that," she reassures.

Someone has to be sacrificed. The game is all that matters. My parents occupy placeholders, phoning it in, expecting me to magically know everything. And if I don't, punishment is swift and harsh. Neither has ever constructively helped me with school.

When I was four, his style of teaching me to read was to whip my hands with a belt—two or three lashes for every missed word until they were red and blistered.

"Hold out your hands you stubborn little bitch."

That's how he talked to me. I didn't know how to answer his questions, because there were so many possibilities. So I stuttered to buy time while my mind jumped between possible scenarios. I always chose wrong.

In fifth grade, he called it "motivation", slapping me hard across the face every time I couldn't remember a times table. I had difficulty concentrating on anything but the hand slapping my face and possible escalation to a beating with the belt. Momma looked the other way, pretended it wasn't happening. And when I most needed understanding—when I most needed a hug, I received physical, verbal, and emotional violence.

Report card days were especially bad. Aaron and I received beatings for grades lower than a C. The back of the book doesn't give answers for odd numbered questions. In a family like this one, Aaron and I are the odd ones out. For mundane things like being alive, the probability of setting him off in a violent lather is 50/50. Odds soar to 100% when engaging him about anything that matters, so I wrack my brain for another hour before admitting defeat. He muddles over the problem, writing and rewriting, scratching out and erasing, until giving up after thirty minutes, but not before abruptly slapping me off the chair onto the floor. He waits for that sweet moment, the one where you're completely off-guard, the one where you think you've gotten off, and then . . . Wham! Water flowing from a faucet—hot and cold—on and off—fire and gasoline—Molotov cocktail and pyromania. There is nothing in between.

"Stop mocking me you little bitch," he screeches. You trying to make me look dumb? You're the one that's too stupid to live! You need to figure out your own goddamned homework!"

The next day Momma coos—"It's really not that bad. Yes, he is a little heavy-handed at times, but he's a good man. Try to stay out of his way. Stop upsetting him. If you don't, he'll take it out on all of us."

What she's really saying is—"Better you than me. Glad it wasn't me this time. No hard feelings." With the bottle safely stashed under my pillow, I go about the day, pretending to be alive . . . homework . . . feed the dog . . . get ready for school. At dinner, I stare at Aaron's split lip, the welts striping his arms and neck, and his downcast eyes on the verge of tears. He was also sacrificed for the game. Everyone pretends not to notice, except me.

He barks orders. "More tea...hot peppers...coffee...dessert!" Momma scurries in an attempt to stave off the imminent explosion. Impossible. I am only thirteen and I know there is no escape. Momma's turn. The fuse is burned to the quick—only a matter of hours, minutes, seconds.

When the house ebbs to white noise, I fill my hand with white tablets and greedily down them between sips of water . . . place the glass on the nightstand because an out of place glass won't matter tomorrow . . . cross my arms over my heart . . . heavy lids. "God, please deliver me from the trap. Let me go into the light." Violent nausea sends me to the toilet half an hour after completing the final act. Between erupting waves of half-digested pills and bile, I lay on the bathroom floor with my swollen cheek against the cold white tiles inhaling the faint smell of Clorox and Pine Sol. When there is nothing left but defeat and bitter aftertaste, I drag back to bed disappointed that I have to live another day.

A loud crack somewhere in the night . . . the clock at the bedside reads 3:02am. Detonation. Slapping . . .

snapping . . . gnashing belt . . . beating . . . crashing . . . pleading . . . crying . . . yelling . . . screaming . . . spitting . . . torture.

"That baby ain't mine you goddamned bitch! Who the hell you been fucking, you whore? I saw you making eyes at Davis. That little black bastard doesn't even look like me!" Slap, slap, crash, slap.

"Cunt, you trying to fool me? You trying to pawn Davis' little bastard off on me, aren't you? Not a one of those little bastards is mine!"

"Stop! You're hurting me! I'm not trying to fool you! I would never do that! I love only you! Please stop! You're hurting me," she pleads.

Her screams fuse with the rhythmic, cringe worthy snap of belt on flesh. Finally, cessation—no more screaming—just broken-hearted sobs.

"Why? Why do you do this to me? I haven't done anything to deserve it," she moans hoarsely. Murmured apologies.

"You know I love you, don't you? You just need to stop provoking me."

It's all over by the time the police knock on the door. But, since they are here, I hope that they will be able to help us this time. Please let this be the time that someone does something. Let this be the time that they recognize how dire the situation really is, and how much pain and fear we live with every day.

Momma hides, won't come out of the room into the open. He smoothes it over—it's all been a terrible mistake. They take his word and leave us to fend for ourselves. I am crestfallen. A dark shadow of hopelessness spreads over the house as I hear the police car pull away.

I run warm water over the ice tray, and crack it. From experience, five is too many, four is just right. I wrap the cubes in a hand towel and place it on the TV tray next to a bowl of Campbell's chicken noodle. Liquids are the only nourishment that can pass through the bulbously swollen lips in the obliterated black and blue face. Both eyes are nearly swollen shut, the left open enough to expose a large hematoma in the sclera . . . red, watery, and angry looking. She's been in bed two days now. I help her shamble to the toilet, wait patiently, then help her back to bed, fluff the pillows, gently lean her back, urge her to eat. The routine takes from 30 to 45 minutes and we repeat it four to five times a day.

When I'm at school, she's on her own. He's been gone since that night, don't know where, don't care, just glad he's not here. He'll be back though. Praying for his demise is a waste of time and energy. I get Momma to sign checks so I can buy food. With no saddlebags for my bike, grocery shopping is a juggling act; one trip for milk, another for lunch meat, bread, spaghetti, sauce mix, hamburger, cigarettes, and coffee. I make lunches, walk the little ones to and from school, cook, and clean house. And, as if my burden isn't heavy enough, Momma holds onto me for emotional ballast. At best, our relationship is psychologically incestuous; one sided for sure, uncomfortable to say the least. I give. She takes. She discloses things that never should be revealed to a child, and I forget that I'm just a little girl because I've never been one.

"I take these beatings so you won't have to grow up in poverty, but he's getting meaner by the day. I don't know if I can take any more. I think he's trying to kill me! Why would he do this to me?"

I want to shout, "What are you asking me for? I'm the kid!"

Instead, I pretend to listen. It's the only semi-positive attention I get. I both want it and resent it, and I am especially resentful that she makes us the reason for staying in violence and dysfunction. In her eyes I am a stupid lump of clay, a caricature, a simpleton. In reality, I am wise beyond my years, and it is no wonder that suicide is a daily thought—a persistent conversation swirling round my head. I live in a world where letting them know I know is dangerous. I have nowhere to go because I exist in isolation, inside a vacuum created by my parent's determination to keep the secret. So, I pretend to be dumb, cooperative, sympathetic, and dead. I tell no one of my plans, especially not them. No other explanation exists for me to still be alive, except that I have a guardian angel. I try pills a few more times with the same result. Once, I even managed to wrestle a Luger to my mouth and pull the trigger. The sucker jammed. All efforts to off myself end in epic fails, and all this while Momma lives in la-la land.

"You're the lucky one, Leanne. One day, you'll leave home and forget all about this," is what she tells me. And oddly, neither of them notices a whole bottle of aspirin is missing.

When I turn sixteen, another epiphany hits like a brick; only two more years to go, may as well wait it out. I stop trying to kill myself and secretly plan an exit strategy.

A study by Yount & Li (2009) found women living inside a household where domestic violence is a normal occurrence have a distorted view of normalcy. As mothers, their management of abuse seems incongruous to the reality of the situation. Instead of protecting their children from the abuser, they model coping strategies like minimizing, denial, and justification. They teach their children that abuse is normal, to accept abuse as a regular occurrence, and that what happens inside the home, no matter how distressing and dangerous, is private. Additionally, as consummate enablers, they manipulate their children's behavior by teaching them to pacify the abuser even when there is a very real danger of injury or death.

A study performed by Dube et al. (2001), found the risk of suicide in a sample population of children exposed to adverse childhood experiences, such as emotional, physical, and sexual abuse, alcohol or drug abuse, mental illness in the household, parental separation, incarcerated household member, or battered mother was high, ranging from 64% to 80% of all attempts. More frequent exposures to the eight categories of abuse listed above were also found to dramatically increase the risk of attempted suicide in childhood, adolescence, or adulthood.

Eleven

Playing the room like a Jesus rock star, Pastor Ball meets, greets, and glad-hands from person-to-person.

"Hello. So sorry to be here on such a sad occasion," he schmoozes.

Socorro controls his interaction with me—makes a quick, almost nonexistent introduction, and then artfully whisks him away. Most people would be insulted by the abrupt interaction. Not me. Go ahead. Be my guest. Introduce me as the 'sister from another mister', or the 'sister from another mother', or the sister from another planet for all I care—won't hurt my feelings. I'm okay with being alien. That short intro was her way of controlling information, her way of saying, "Don't betray the family. Play the game!" My prolonged absences tell a story they don't want told, one they want to deny, but can't. I don't do what they want. One by one, my sisters ask why I didn't bring Omar.

"He wants to spend time with his dad," I deflect.

They don't understand my need to protect my son from the family sickness. They don't get that Javier and I are partners, and that he is a capable, loving parent, and I am filled with relief when I think of the two of them hanging out together while I'm here.

Ruben is next to take command of the pastor's attentions. Heads bowed in a huddle of intense conversation, prayer maybe? I'm not sure. I can't help but notice how unkind the years have been, how they have out and out kicked his ass. Lookin' like death warmed over, standin' on a street corner, eatin' on a soda cracker. Stifling a giggle at the visual, my eyes bore straight through him. Aaron would have thought it was funny, too.

Just as quickly, amusement is replaced with pangs of loss and regret. He is the specter of death standing on a street corner in the dark—skeletal, stooped, sunken cheeked, probably weighing 145 pounds. He is dying. That much is obvious.

When I was a kid, he was fearsome; broad, squared off shoulders, nipped in waist, exceptionally fit, 6'2", 185 pounds, movie star good looks, nice dresser—this confirmed by almost everyone we knew. You see, people have special expectations of beautiful people, and he fit the bill perfectly. They were rapt, blind to the underbelly of this brutally cruel man. When he did mean things right in front of them, they chose to look the other way. Instead of speaking up, they made excuses for his behavior, just as my mother had. He was smart enough to surround himself with the easily fooled. The situation was made more confusing by Momma's reactions. She made excuses for his behavior, but never missed an opportunity to bad-mouth him behind his back to his children. Top, that's what his men called him—the revered and feared 1st sergeant, the giver of verbal karate chops, drop and gimme a hundreds, and in your face chewin' outs; tear down and build up the Army way. His job description was warrior and it was his job to train young warriors. For his fervor, he was rewarded with special training in the art of warfare—hand-to-hand combat, sniping, subduing, containing threats, and techniques of torture. Aaron, Momma, and I were his preferred enemies. Nonetheless, the military wasn't responsible for the sadistic behavior he exhibited.

Double-edged sword, conundrum, quandary, dilemma, pickle, predicament are descriptors that readily come to mind. If not for the Sword of Damocles cutting both ways, life for us would have been far, far worse. The military simply provided a legitimate outlet for his aggression and killing instinct. When the cops come to your house almost every week to break up the violence, people begin to talk. So right after I graduated from high school, he moved us to Sand Springs where Gram and his brothers still live. Our family of eight went from living in a five bedroom, three bath custom-built house to a two bedroom apartment. Because of the Freedom Plan, I rolled over and landed on my feet, got a job, enrolled in summer school at Tulsa Community College, and kept it moving.

One of the great things about living in Sand Springs was staying at Gram's house any time I wanted. She loved having me around, and I loved being with her. Oddly, neither of my parents objected because she was older and they thought she could use the company. Aaron and I practically moved in with her. I'd stop at her house at least four times a week for a sleepover, and we'd stay up into the night talking and laughing. When it came time for bed, she'd pull a freshly laundered nightgown from her bureau for me to wear. It smelled of her and her smell enveloped me in love. We'd drink hot chocolate and talk until one of us fell asleep. She gave Aaron and me a place of respite from Momma and Ruben's craziness. She dearly loved all of her grandchildren, and we adored her. She was the one person in our lives who loved us unconditionally.

We'd been in Sand Springs a month when one of Ruben's girlfriends showed up on the doorstep of their apartment pretending she just happened to be in the neighborhood. I'll call her Carol. Carol was married and had two young children. But she packed her clothes into a huge suitcase and left her husband and children in El Paso to crowd into Ruben and Momma's small apartment. The tension was palpable. I came and went, mostly went, but when stopping in for clothes, or to bring cigarettes and coffee, Momma followed me around asking, "Why is that woman in my house?"

"Why are you asking me," I'd respond. "You know why she's here, Momma!"

"What are you talking about? I don't know why that woman's invited herself to stay in my house," she challenges crossly.

One day, I came for clothes and Carol was gone. Ruben became angry and terse again. The beatings and abuse started anew.

His brother Robert saw how fearful we were, and confronted him, but that was like waving a red cape in front of a bull. Ruben grabbed me by the throat soon after their confrontation. He had a murderous look in his eyes.

"Did you talk to Robert about me? Cause if you did, I'm going to beat the shit out of you right here and now!"

"No," I lie.

Soon afterward I learned that the demon of domestic violence runs in the family, and that Uncle Robert was also one of its perpetrators. At breakfast one morning, Gayla (that's Uncle Robert's wife) burst through the front door screaming, "He's going to kill me! Help me!" She dove under the kitchen table just as Robert appeared in the open doorway. We scattered. He gave chase, moving the heavy table this way and that as though it were cardboard. He slid the table to one side. She crawled to the opposite end just out of reach, all the while screaming—"Help me! Please, help me!" The sound of her screams and the dragging of heavy wood on the floor filled the small space. Shockingly, Ruben was the one to step in and stop the melee.

"You can't beat your wife in my house. Keep it at home, man!"

The only problem was that he hadn't kept the violence contained behind closed doors.

The walls are closing in. I can't breathe. A panic attack threatens. Promising escape is the front door and I am transported through its portal. Standing in the shade keeps the sun's full glare at bay. Every now and then passing cars stir wispy ghosts and scuttling leaves into little dervishes. Having broken free of the Earth-bound body that failed him, Aaron's spirit floats on gentle breezes.

"It's going to be all right, Leanne. I'm okay now," he whispers. He was the only male born to Ruben and Arianne Foushée, and we clicked from day one. I adore him and that adoration is returned. People say one name—finish with the other—Aaron and Leanne—Leanne and Aaron. I am wise beyond my years, so level-headed at ten years old that I regularly babysit my younger siblings—Aaron eight, Jewel seven, Socorro five, Anna almost three. Although Momma's not showing, I suspect she's pregnant again because the beatings are more frequent and vicious than normal. For me, the negative fallout increases with every passing year . . . no hugs, encouragement, or loving words... just more responsibility for the younger ones as Momma gives birth to their latest baby. When the bloom is off the rose, and the newness has worn off last year's model, she becomes disinterested, and it's time for a new one. When their relationship deteriorates, they have another baby to make it better because everyone knows that adding a new child to the mix keeps everyone tied to their roles. I am so beaten down I can't see any good in myself. My friends are loneliness, despair, and sadness. I am a rat on a running wheel, spinning, spinning, spinning.

One of my maternal aunts referred to me as the little girl with heavy, adult responsibilities.

"You were too young to be so burdened. You held it together, though. I admired your spunk. I admired you."

I am still a tad shocked, uncomfortable, a little embarrassed even when people show me what I looked like through their eyes because I had no connection to that person. While everyone else saw me as a scrappy, tenacious survivor, I saw a useless, bungling, and hopeless incompetent. And while my parents assumed it was my job to take care of their children, they never had anything positive to say to me, or about me. But Aaron touched my whimsy with his quick wit and mischievous sparkle. If there was impishness to be had, we found it together. I wanted to be more like him, not the weary old woman I was.

After putting the little ones to bed, he holds the phone in the air. "I dare ya," he goads. We drool like idiots in devilish, giggling fits interrupted only by the inability to draw breath, and the time it takes to dial another number. We hold our stomachs to keep from bursting with tears streaming down our faces in pure unadulterated glee.

"Hello, this is Joe's repair. I understand your washer needs fixin'. Our man will be there tomorrow around 8:00am—the butt crack of dawn!" Sometimes they hang up after the butt crack comment, but sometimes they don't.

"But I didn't call a repair man," comes the next answer.

That means they've taken the bait.

"Oh! Are you sure no one called?"

"Yes, I'm quite sure."

"Oh dear! There's been a terrible mix-up. Maybe, it could be a circuit. Are your lights on?"

"Why, yes."

"Is your refrigerator running?"

"Let me check. Yes, it's running."

"Then you'd better go catch it!"

We hang up squealing with gales of laughter. The next sketch involves letting Prince Albert out of the can. I'm actually smiling when Arianne pokes her head out the door.

"Are you looking for me?" "Yeah, it's time."

With most everyone's eyes intent on the pastor, we join in a bubble of intimacy. Don't cry here. Not here! I focus on anything but the loss of my beloved brother—the flowers, the wall color, the photograph. Kindness, optimism, youth, and beauty, mixed with a spark of intelligence, that's what I see. I gaze searchingly into his eyes for some hidden answer, some hidden meaning, some clue missed along the way. The truth is neatly secreted away, nothing on the surface that would foretell the future, but I am now sure it was there all along. Thoughtful, positive, measured, non-denominational—a pinch of Buddhism—a smattering of Judaism—a little New Age spirituality thrown in for good measure—not at all what I expected from the Bible Belt. A prayer. Bowed heads. It's over. Almost immediately, Ruben's party mode laughter infiltrates my thoughts. He's drawn an audience; me included. I study his gestures, his facial expressions, the way he talks, the way he laughs. He looks up, catches me staring, and for a split second we lock eyes before he blinks and looks away. Everyone notices. The room quiets . . . all eyes on us. Awkward! Rumors about us having bad blood are now confirmed. Whispers.

"You know they haven't spoken in a decade?"
"Why, what happened?"
"Don't know."

Time passes. Morning turns to afternoon, afternoon to sunset. This time, the patio door beckons. Sitting in a lawn chair, I watch stars blink into view. Wind chimes of laughter and conversation tinkle in the background. A star falls from the sky so suddenly I wonder if I'm seeing things. Technically, it fell long before the light reached the sky above Earth so I could see it fall.

Twelve

It's my way or the highway, he often said. I preferred the highway so I ran away pretty frequently, once managing to avoid capture for five days and four nights. Slithering out the bedroom window and stealing away into the inky night with six dollars of hard earned babysitting money in my pocket, a blanket, some food, and water in my backpack, I made a break for it. Destination: The Annex, a military recreation center. My plan is to sleep in one of the bathrooms, but they are locked up tight, so that first night is spent with my back against an outbuilding—hunkered down in the pitch-black—listening to the shrilling winds. Sand grains buffet the building in staccato making it difficult to determine whether the dry husking in the bushes is a scuttling animal, or a serial killer who's found his next victim. Squatting low to the ground and pulling the blanket tightly around me, I huddle within the desert's impersonal embrace, weeping in despair between fits of shivering, and episodes of head nodding micro-sleep and nightmares. The desert is no more impersonal than my human mother and father, but she keeps my confidence and I both love and hate her for it.

At dawn, the sun squints above the horizon. By noon, 100° temperatures drive me out of hiding long enough to fill my canteen from a water fountain. The rest of the long hours are spent hugging the shade side of a ravine. Around six, the winds begin to surge, bringing an urgent need for shelter from the cold of the coming night. I decide to make an hour's hike to an outdoor mall at the desert's edge. Hiking alone in the desert is never safe. In fact, it's downright dangerous even for the most skilled survivalist. And because there are no manmade landmarks at the midway point, the only visual cues are almost imperceptible animal trails, a cairn of boulders, the personality of the cacti, and the position of the Franklin mountain range over my right shoulder. Read wrong, I could become lost, wandering in an endless loop for agonizing days before keeling over and shriveling up into a desiccated husk. Creatures that call the desert home have succumbed to its deadly embrace. Along the dusty trail I come across bleached bones under black feathers; a scrap of fur snagged in stinkweed; a rabbit skull with vacant eyes scoured clean by fire ants. I keep moving until arriving at the massive sand dune buttressing a cement retaining wall the purpose of which is to protect the city from drifting sand. Slowly, but surely, the desert is reclaiming her territory. As the sun sinks behind the mountains, I shift down the dune to the other side, and spend a few moments pouring sand from my shoes. The sun is almost gone. The mall is a football field away. Hoping not to step on a rattler lazing across the warm ground, I make a mad dash into gusting wind, every stride a fight for breath. By the time I wrestle the steel door of the dank little restroom open and flip on the light, it's dark. I'm done in. Sweat beads glisten on my forehead. Blood pounds at my temples, rushes in my ears so loudly; I can barely hear my jagged breathing bounce off filthy, graffiti covered walls. Exhaustion and little sleep from the night before leaves little room to quibble over germs. I lock the door, spread out the blanket, tuck my pack under my head, and fall fast asleep without turning the light off.

On day five near sundown, the cops catch me breaking across the field. And just like that, I'm bumping along in the backseat of a police cruiser on my way to back to pandemonium. They don't really give a shit about me. Why keep calling the cops to bring me back? While I'm gone Ruben and Momma have to be responsible for their own kids. No screeching my name when the dishes need doing, the bathrooms need cleaning, the laundry needs washing, or dinner needs to be made—the list is endless. And if Momma needs care after a beating, or my siblings need someone to take care of them, I haven't been available. One of the officers cocks his head in my general direction.

"Why did you run away," he asks. Something must be very wrong at home that you would keep running away. What is it? That should be the question. But he has no real concern for why I would trade the warmth of a house for the cold of the desert night. He doesn't want to know why I prefer to sleep in a nasty public restroom. And I'm not stupid enough to volunteer any information. Dejavu! I've been here before. They won't believe me because Ruben's job as 1st sergeant makes his word unimpeachable. They'll tell him what I've said. He'll give some song and dance about how I'm out of control. They'll nod knowingly while dusting their hands of the situation. Once they're down the road out of earshot he'll beat the crap out of me for embarrassing him. No, it's best to keep my mouth shut. I'm in enough trouble as it is, so I mumble something about needing a vacation. As difficult as they've been, the past few days have been a retreat.

He skillfully maneuvers the chess pieces around the board, sings the same song—monochromatic notes in perfect pitch with textures of righteous indignation, sprinkled with a smattering of phony concern.

"You ran away because of your Momma, didn't you? Didn't you," he yells, while stabbing me in the chest with an index finger. He does this right in front of the cops.

I want to explode, "It's because I'm afraid of you. It's because I never know when you'll blow. You're the one who beats the crap out of us! You're the one who's dangerous and scary!"

He doesn't want an answer, and he sure as hell doesn't want the truth. Maybe it won't go so badly for me if I keep my mouth shut. The next day, Momma blames my running away on him.

"I know it's his fault you ran away," she accuses.

Thirteen

We didn't have a pot to piss in or a window to throw it out of. Momma loved to make colloquial statements like this one. The window, and the pot filled with piss was one of her favorites. Not having a pot to piss in, or a window to through it out of was an allegory about growing up poor on a farm without indoor plumbing; hence the need for a pot to piss in. The window was a metaphor for the missing pieces of her life. No window, no introspection.

I settle into a window seat. A fellow passenger takes the aisle—nods acknowledgement. I do the same in a way that says, I don't want to engage. The pilot announces that the plane will be full, but the middle seat remains empty the entire flight. I imagine him sitting next to me. As the flight attendants begin to circulate the cabin taking drink orders and handing out stale cheese crackers, the sleeplessness of recent weeks catches up. I close my eyes and float away.

At 13, he mows lawns for cash even though allergies render him virtually non-functional by evening; however nothing stops him from making money for fireworks . . . not headaches, red, watery eyes, or a perpetually runny nose. Momma and Ruben believe his allergies are faked to garner sympathy. As far as their concerned, allergies are a figment of the imagination.

"Only white folks can afford allergies," is what Momma used to say. "They don't exist. Stop sniffling, and stop using all the toilet paper to blow your nose," she commanded irritably.

June 15th is opening day for Boomtown, and until closing day on July 5th, he makes at least two hour-long round trips, sometimes with a posse, and sometimes alone. Pedaling fast, he rounds the corner. It's obvious where he's been. The rumpled brown paper bag bobbing against the handlebar is full of fireworks.

"Hey! I got black cats! Wanna come with?"

The delight in his voice is tempting. I want to tag along.

"I can't. I have to watch the little kids," I yell at his back as he and his cadre zips past on the way to the desert.

Sometimes Aaron escapes. Not me. I am rarely given permission to leave the house because I'm always on call. And besides, girls aren't allowed to just take off like that. There are two sets of rules, one for males, and another for females. Females are for washing dishes, cleaning and cooking, doing the laundry, and preparing to be the next generation of victim. "You didn't see me," he shouts into the wind. Ruben found an excuse later that same day. "Have you seen him?" he demands.

"No," I lie.

"Find him! Tell him to get his ass home right damn now if he knows what's good for him," he yells.

He's hanging at the Annex, jumping on the trampolines.

"Pops is looking for you and he's on the rampage," I warn.

"You know, Leanne, I love everything about summer . . . no school . . . riding my bike . . . sneaking out at night . . . staying in the desert until sun up. I love all of it, except him."

"I know, Aaron. Me too."

When he got back that evening, Ruben beat him until his back bled. It wasn't the first time, nor would it be the last, but this time I couldn't be like Momma and pretend it wasn't happening. His anguished screams filled the house. I couldn't stick my head in the sand. If no one intervened he was going to die. So, I timidly opened the door. Balled up in fetal position on the floor, hands and elbows covering his head. He squirms this way and that to out-maneuver the belt. Ruben swings it from high overhead, brings it down on his back again and again. The bloodletting sprays castoff from Aaron's soul all over the walls and ceiling.

"Please stop, Poppa! You're killing him!" Trancelike, rage-aholic, sweaty, crazed, wall-eyed, dilated pupils filled with hatred, he can't hear me. He's in the zone. Louder this time, "Please stop. You're killing him!"

Slowly he climbs out of the hole. His head swivels toward me. There is nothing human in the eyes.

"Get out," he growls. "I know what I'm doing you dumb little bitch! Shut that goddamned door before I beat the shit out of you too! Get out!"

In a quavering voice, I continue to plead even though I'm not feeling too good about what's next. In a split second, he leaves Aaron on the floor, crosses the room, grabs me by the throat and cracks me so hard across the face I slide backwards through the doorway. Before my foot is completely clear of the threshold, the door slams, pinching the toe of my sneaker in the jamb. I sit disoriented—inner ear ringing as the brutal assault continues. Pulling my shoe free leaves a half-moon of dirty rubber sole behind. I'm going to be in trouble when he sees my shoe, is all I can think. When it's quiet, I am conscious of a steady tinny ringing in my ears.

The next day Momma comes at me in anger. "What is wrong with you? Stop provoking him! Don't you know how to keep your damn mouth shut and stay out of his way? The next time you aggravate him like that, I'm going to knock your teeth down your throat my damn self!" She slaps me hard across the face and then strikes me with the belt she's been holding in her left hand. Slap. Belt, Slap. Belt. But I'm bigger than her, so I catch the end of the belt and rip it away from her leaving her standing there blinking in disbelief.

"You're such a hypocrite! You're not supposed to let him beat Aaron like that! And I'm not going take beatings from both of you! Fuck you," I yell slamming the door on the way out. I throw the belt into a drainage ditch at the end of the block and disappear for two days before being caught and brought back.

Inhaling the fragrance of pungent desert flowers and scrub brush, we lay side-by-side on a boulder, watching the clouds change shapes in a memory of warm sun on upturned faces. He slides off and begins turning over stones like I'd seen him do so many times before. Mission accomplished, he climbs back up and places a horned toad in my palm. Its wide, plated head, stubby tail, flat scaly body sends me back to a time when lizards and snakes and desert crawly things filled him with wonder. He made a whimsical habitat in a large shallow box under his bed for his lizards, hand-fed them crickets and flies, read books about them, made lifelike drawings of them. But that was over the day Momma danced on the sofa shrieking blood and murder after coming across the one named Charlie bobbing up and down on the living room carpet.

"Do you remember," he asks with a coltish grin spreading across his face. "Yeah," I giggle.

He takes me to the backyard of a house in which we lived when I was nine, and he was seven. "I had some of the best times of my life here. Do you remember?" he asks.

I nod. Almost every morning after breakfast during the summer, Momma parked us in the backyard cubicle of cement mortar and stone like we were puppies.

"Don't come back in until I call you," she warns as she pulls the door closed and locks it. We can see her through the picture window enjoying the air conditioning, and if she's not sitting on the couch in front of the TV watching her Soaps, drinking coffee and smoking cigarettes, she's asleep. If the little ones need to go potty, it is my job to negotiate their reentry, straight to the bathroom and out again. I hate waking her because she gets so angry. When she doesn't get off the couch quickly enough, I point out a hidden spot in the bushes for them to relieve themselves. We drink water from the hose and eat vegetables from the garden. And, although I am responsible for them, Aaron and I manage to live inside a fantasy made of imagination and escape. Our troll dolls climb treacherous mountain paths on the wall to caves made of broken rock. What would it be like to be free like those trolls?

The children fade to the two of us in the present as adults. Reaching into the darkness of a crevice, my fingers touch something. Dirty and weatherworn, the little doll's green hair is filled with leaves and dried grass—a memory suspended in time for more than forty years. In it, Ruben's recently returned from Vietnam—a homecoming filled with anxiety, grief, dread, fear, confusion, sadness. Socorro was born during his absence. A couple of weeks after walking through the door, he is beating Momma behind the closed door of their bedroom while screaming at her for being unfaithful. Aaron, Jewel, and I sit on the floor of a closet, clinging to each other helplessly listening to the baby crying, Momma's tortured screams, and Ruffo's nervous barking. Before Vietnam, Ruffo had been his dog, but now every time he sees the man he used to worship, he cowers in fear and barks in fear.

That day, with crystal clarity, in a gesture symbolizing the official end of childhood, I left my beloved troll in the cave. That awareness had been mounting for some time like paper clips strung together in a continuous chain, and wound around a Christmas tree. Every violent event added another link to the chain until it became unwieldy, unmanageable, untenable, and uncontrollable. It snaked round my neck, pinning my arms to my sides, gagging my mouth, and keeping the outside world from discovering my secret shame, my secret prison. When I was three we lived in Colorado Springs. Trudging beside him, we head toward the tall metal slide in the little playground behind Base Quarters. What should be a joyous event is more like going to an execution.

"Just let go," he demands. I hesitate. "I'll catch you, you goddamned fraidy cat! Just-let-go! If I have to come up there and get you, I'm going to tear your little ass up," he explodes.

It is not because of some joyful glee or thrill that I let go. I let go because I am more afraid of him than falling from the slide. I let go because I want his love. I let go because I love my Poppa and want him to be happy with me. He busts me in the mouth, knocks me off my feet into the dirt.

"Stop sucking your tongue you damn dummy! How many times do I have to tell you?"

Salty, metallic tang seeps onto my tongue. I want to cry, but he'll hit me again, so I suck it up.

"I'm gonna break you of that habit, if it's the last thing I do. You better not cry, or I'll have to shut that fat mouth up for you," he rants.

Momma tries to explain it away. "You were about two months old when I had to leave you with Gram for three weeks. I didn't want to go because I was breastfeeding, but I had no choice. He made me. He said it would be all right. Gram had to feed you from a cup because you wouldn't drink from a bottle. By the time I got back, my milk had dried up. You tried to suck your thumb, but he swatted your hand away. That's when you started sucking your tongue. He seemed to hate you so. I never understood it.

"When my son was one, Momma brought up how helpless she was in yet another excuse filled monologue—the same one I'd heard all my life, And on that day I decided I'd had enough.

"I'm a mom now, and I can't imagine allowing some man beat my helpless babies! I was only a baby, and a stressed out one at that because there was nothing but craziness coming from my parents! What he wanted was unnatural. And what did he know anyway? He was an idiot! You were the mother! You were supposed to protect us! I was there! I went through it! I no longer want to hear how bad it was for you because you could have stopped it by not taking him back."

Finally, after a long pause she answers. "I don't know how to answer that."

"Then stop whining about how you had no choice! Your children were the only ones who had no choice. Stop with the excuses!"

While growing up in chaos, I craved equilibrium and longed for sanity. I didn't exactly know how people were different because that was all I'd known. I just felt there was something very crucial missing, something very off in my family. To compensate, I lied through omission. I lied because I was not allowed to tell the truth. I lied because of shame. I lied because I wanted to believe in the fairytale, but the truth was literally and figuratively slapping me in the face. It would be embarrassing for friends to find out. And that is why I rarely invited anyone into the inner sanctum. I attempted to ignore the truth only once when I was twelve.

I finally made a friend at school. Her name is Midge. Not long afterward, her sister Katrina returns from ballet training in Germany. I met her as well and the two embrace me. Katrina is beautiful and modern and I look up to her. She attends college and teaches ballet and modern jazz in the evenings at a local recreation center. She and Midge invite me to come with, and I am ecstatic. Thursday evenings, just the three of us in Katrina's beat up VW bug. I love ballet . . . excel at it. Six months in, Ruben tells me I can't go unless I take my sisters along. Jewel is nine; Socorro is eight; Anna is five; Arianne is four. I ask Katrina if it's all right to bring them along. She says yes. We go in her car, but she soon tells me her car is too small to accommodate everyone, so my parents will have to get us there, from here on out. The reality hits me hard. I don't drive, but that's not obvious to my parents, and I can't ask them to be parents—out of the question—just not going to happen. There is no other way out of the dilemma, so I quit.

Ruben gloats by saying, "You see? Those white folks don't give a shit about you! Even they see you for the worthless piece of shit you really are."

Midge invites me to her house often, but I am reluctant to return the invitation. One day, she asks why.

"It's only fair," she asserts.

She's right. I hope this one time it will be okay. Maybe, he won't be at the house and, if he is, maybe he will be in a good mood. This is highly unlikely though, and I know it. Maybe, I can fly under the radar—unlikely as well. Maybe, maybe, maybe! All I need is a couple of hours. So, on a sunny Saturday afternoon, Midge arrives, dropped off by her mom. That morning, before her arrival, we performed the routine of cleaning the house from top to bottom, scuttling like little mice to right anything out of place before he could find any fault. Notching up the fear a click with each passing minute, he growls, threatens, scowls, pushes, shoves, berates. Nothing we did was right. Nothing we ever did was good enough. Detonation was imminent. I know it. Momma knows it.

After the work is done, Aaron disappears, probably to the desert, and I am left regretting a childish lapse. I cloister Midge in my bedroom with Arianne, Anna, and Ruffo. We talk and joke. And, just like ballet, it is all taken away. He calls Momma with that tone. As they pass down the hall, Midge whispers, "What's wrong?" It's glaringly obvious that something is about to explode.

I've been holding my breath. Letting out a slow exhalation gives me some time to formulate a distraction. "Oh, nothing," I lie quickly. Hoping to avoid it by not being inside the house, I suggest we go outside. On the front porch, we sit in lawn chairs hidden behind trellises of delicately fragranced yellow and pink roses. Light breezes bring in the pungency of thorny desert flowers—and ozone. The tension is written on my face.

What's wrong," Midge asks again. "I'm n-n-n-not sure," I stutter, but before I can get the rest of the lie out of my mouth, Momma bursts from the house to sit next to me. She's clutching her purse, and breathlessly sobbing. He explodes after her, gruffly snatches the purse, grabs her arm, and violently wrestles her back into the house, damaging the screen door in the process. Although he was nowhere to be found when it happened, Aaron got the beating for the broken door. In this house, damaged doors and holes in the walls are regularly blamed on the children, usually Aaron. It's like they can't remember what transpires but, more than likely, finding a scapegoat is the way to put the incidences into another compartment.

"Get your ass back in here," he commands.

The color drains from Midge's face. "I need to call my mom now," she croaks in a dry, trembling whisper.

Of course, she does. This is my normal, not hers. My parents are delusionists who honestly don't know that they are fucking wolves. Here's the rule I need to get around in order to grant Midge that phone call. The house phone is off limits when he's berserk for obvious reasons. No calling outsiders for help! Their bedroom is at the end of the hall in direct view of the phone stand when the door is open. I plan the logistics. He raises his voice. I grab her hand. The door slams. I both pull and drag her down the hall, and wait anxiously for her to nervously dial and redial the number.

In a tiny voice, "Mommy, will you come get me?" A pause. I can't hear the conversation on the other end over the beating taking place a few feet away, but I can tell her mom is asking, "What's wrong?"

"Mommy, please hurry. Come get me now," she repeats urgently.

We move back outside to wait for her mom to arrive. As the war rages on in the background, she sits rigidly, scanning the street. I apologize, but she can't hear me. When the big green 88 pulls to the curb, Midge bolts at a dead run. Needless to say, she never asks to come to my house again.

On Monday, Ruben comes home from work, grabs me by the throat, pins me against the wall, and chokes me while accusing me of telling Midge what goes on inside his house. It turns out Midge's dad was his Commanding Officer and Midge, as she should have, went straight home and told her parents. Ruben forbids me from seeing her because now it's my fault he showed his ass. I visited Midge and her family a couple of times after the incident, but couldn't handle the looks of pity. It was just easier not to have friends.

I'm squeezing his hand now. "I don't want to remember this, Aaron. Why am I thinking about this? It should stay buried."

"But, you were the brave one, Leanne. I looked up to you."

"You've got it all wrong. I was a coward. I ran away as fast as my legs could carry me."

He pauses, thoughtfully measures his words before speaking again.

"I waited until it was too late. He broke me. I should have run, too. You can't please them and please yourself at the same time. Impossible! There's no straddling the fence. Either you're in or out."

I twitch awake as the pilot announces the final approach to Oakland International.

Kilpatrick and Williams (1998) found that children who witness Domestic Violence (DV) are susceptible to developing Post-Traumatic Stress Disorder (PTSD) in later life. Adult survivors exhibit PTSD symptoms in three categories, or combinations thereof. First, they can re-experience the trauma just like veterans of combat. The second is an avoidance of feeling the psychological trauma, also known as psychological numbing. And the third is increased agitation that was not present before traumatic event occurred.

Fourteen

I vowed never to marry, or to have kids, but that was before meeting Javier. I also vowed not to blindly follow in their footsteps because as role models go, I was not impressed. There was also a practical reason for those vows. I had difficulty letting my guard down because, when you come from a family like mine, trust is an ill afforded commodity. And an intimate relationship requires trust. But Javier turned out to be home from the moment we met . . . kind, gentle, steadfast, loving, loyal. And oh, how I tested him expecting him to come out his bag and show his true self. He was/is genuine, the real deal.

California became our home together—a place for creating all the things missed, all the things stolen from me in childhood—a place far, far from my origins. The age-old adage, home is where the heart is, best describes it. I am content. I am loved and respected. Over the years, Momma tries to pull me back into the fold. "We haven't seen you in awhile," she'll say. "You need to come home." Trading bedlam for this life isn't going to happen. I don't feel the need to visit more often than I do. So as not to hurt her feelings, I make excuses.

"I don't have the money. I have to work. I'll try to make it soon."

All lies. It's funny how she expects me to protect her reality, and how I sometimes still do. What I really wanted to say is, "Home? What home are you talking about? Home would be a place filled with fond memories, a haven from the stresses of the world, a place of safety and security, a place where I won't be ambushed, or abused." The home she speaks of is only in her imagination. In my reality, lurking behind the door is an overfed pink elephant defecating in the middle of the room, wearing a Mohawk, Converse All-Star high tops, ripped, punked out t-shirt, and rusted safety pin earrings.

Yet, everyone is supposed to sit around sedately drinking tea with pinkies in the air, pretending he's not there. How can they not see him? The noise he makes is indescribable! It's so loud I have to yell over the trumpeting. "YOU HEAR THAT, RIGHT? WHAT? YOU DON'T SMELL IT EITHER? ARE YOU SURE? CERTAINLY, YOU CAN SEE IT!" Calmly, robotically, in unison they answer: "What elephant? We don't see no stinkin' elephant."

I pull into the garage around midnight. Javier's waited up. He takes my bag into the house. We talk while I unpack. "How was it?" he asks.

"The same," I answer. "Just did my time and got the hell out of there." We laugh.

"Omar tried to wait up for you."

"I'll be happy to see him. I missed you both." A long, hot shower . . . then down the hall to kiss my slumbering little boy on the cheek . . . set the clock . . . and fall into bed next to my beloved . . . asleep before my head hits the pillow . . . dreaming . . . remembering.

At the end of a long corridor stands an ornately carved cabinet. Emitting a long, lazy creak, the butterfly doors swing open.

Behind me, he whispers, "Go ahead. Look at it."

I timidly step closer and peer into the darkness. An assortment of packages in various colors and sizes clutter the shelves. All the way in the back, light reflects from one small box. It's adorned with a perfect gold bow and wrapped in white fabric. Pushing the others aside, I reach for it. The card tucked under the tape reads, "For you, Leanne."

On a warm Sunday morning, the hair stands up on the back of my neck. Tendrils of psychic energy course through my body. The smell of ozone is crisp. My soul escapes, hovers in a corner to watch its body go through the motions of setting the dining room table. The last thing to do is fling the drapes open at the picture window showcasing our 'House Beautiful' to the rest of the world. Passersby are treated to a snapshot of what they wish they had; the perfect family engaged in the perfect breakfast. "It's time to eat," Momma announces. Nervously, everyone sits. We wait for the signal—that it's okay to eat. Without it, we do nothing.

Detonation! Explosion! The scene is laid waste with an upended table that narrowly misses the baby in the high chair. A child's finger-painting of food drips from the wall. Grape juice and milk, sausage, bacon, and scrambled eggs are strewn all over the floor. Unsure of what to do next, my body is frozen, stunned by the percussion blast.

"I can't find my goddamned brush! And one of you little bastards has it! If you know what's good for you, you'd better get your asses up from there now and go find it, or I'm gonna kill every last one of you!" Chair scraping dissolves into frenzy. I run to the back bathroom where it usually resides. I look under the hamper, in the hamper, in the medicine cabinet. Everyone crawls on hands and knees looking through closets, under beds and inside nightstands.

It is not uncommon to find his stash of joints at the bottom of the hamper because one of my endless responsibilities is washing and folding the laundry every other day. I guess he's so high by bedtime he just plain forgets where he's hidden his drugs—or brush for that matter. Minutes of frantic searching go by before Aaron puts the brush in my hand.

"I found it in the closet in one of his boots," he whispers. "Will you take it to him?"

Everyone looks to me to solve the problems. I'm fourteen and I'm scared and I want to run and I want to hide. I need someone to protect and love me, but my role is to draw fire, diffuse, deflect, buffer, absorb, outthink. I am the chosen one—chosen to help the so-called adults play out unfinished family business—chosen by my sisters and brother as the demilitarized zone between them and Ruben and Momma—chosen as the stabilizing leg of the tripod because, sadly, neither Ruben nor Momma combined make a whole person. There's no such thing as direct resolution or solution-oriented communication, honesty, caring, kindness, or accepting responsibility. What we have are complex, convoluted, talk-arounds, symbolic diversions, lies, deceptions, and denials. They think one way. I think another. They need an interactive audience and we're it. Sometimes I feel like the crazy one. Ruben tries to break me by tauntingly calling me the Case, short for mental case. Every time he walks past me, he tells me I'm the ugliest damn thing he's ever seen with my pock marked, acne ridden face. He says I look like a haint because a haint is what there ain't. How could he talk? His skin was acne scarred worst than mine could ever be!

"Momma, I don't want to do this. I didn't take it and besides, you know this stupid brush is not the real reason he's doing this!"

Hot potato, hot potato, who's got the hot potato? Damn it all to hell! It's me!

"Well, you found it," she replies weakly. No one is going to step forward, and who can blame them? Before taking the long walk down the hall to the kitchen where he's waiting for the sacrificial lamb, I look her dead in the eyes and fight back the only way I know how.

"This isn't right and you know it! You're supposed to protect me, not the other way around!"

She looks down at her feet, won't meet my gaze, and says nothing. In my mind's eye, she's sticking her thumbs in her ears shouting, "La, la, la, la! I can't hear you!"

Narratives about her own abysmal childhood give some insight into why she is the way she is. I try to keep that in mind. Her father worked all day and didn't want to know what went on at home while he was away. Her mother had no use for children under foot all day, so she taught them to lie and say they were five when they were actually four, so she could send them off to first grade. Momma's real age was a secret, and if she messed up by telling the truth, she was punished with physical violence. Lies were valued more than the truth. The pressure for a four year-old must have been unimaginable and I'm sure this was one of the psychological abuses that indelibly shaped her life. Her father died when she was thirteen. Momma's eldest sister, Charisma, stepped in to care for and protect her siblings from an abusive mother. My mother was supposed to protect me because she was now the adult but, instead, she remained the scared little girl needing Charisma's protection.

"Mother was always mad after she got home from work, always looking for an excuse to beat us, but Charisma got the worst of it because she was the oldest."

Charisma's not here to save her anymore, so she shoves me out front to shield her from Ruben, the present day embodiment of her abusive, violent mother. And like Charisma, I'm the one getting the worst of it because, not only am I her protective big sister, I am also the protective big sister for my siblings. Funny, how that birth order thing works out. Not only that, Momma allows her children to be beaten just like her father allowed her mother to beat her.

Ruben was the first-born of four brothers and his father died when he was fourteen. Back in the day, the eldest male was expected to take over the father's job of supporting the family, so Ruben was forced to assume financial responsibility for his mother and younger brothers. When convenient, which was most of the time, he assigned that role to me by making me responsible for the actions of my mother and my siblings.

"You're supposed to take care of your sisters and brother. It's up to you because your Momma is incapable. She's dumb as a sack of rocks, too stupid for words, just plain irresponsible. You should know better because you're the oldest," is what he said to me.

My thoughts were; no, that's not true. You and Momma are the oldest. Then because of the broken record playing in his head, he dumped his burdens onto me and he, in turn, used violence to be emotionally distant and unavailable. The set up was all so complicated and twisted and yet, so simple and inevitable. Is there no wonder the two of them found each other?

I'm delicate looking, small-boned, skinny, ninety pounds soaking wet, much of it muscle, and that's a good thing because being fit probably saved me from permanent physical injury. I'm deathly afraid of the hulking cruel man who is my father. A vein pulses at his temple. He snatches the brush from my hand.

"Where did you find it," he demands. "In—in—your c-c-closet," I stammer.

"You goddamned kids better learn to keep your hands off my shit! The next time I can't find my brush, I'm going to walk out on this family and never come back, just like my dad did!" The next thing I remember is waking up on the floor with my face stinging.

"Get your ass up from there and go get ready for church," he orders.

The dead look in his eyes is incentive enough to do as I'm told. I stagger to my feet. An hour and a half later, we are in church, sitting in the front pew, dressed like a basket of pastel Easter eggs, perfectly stair-stepped from the oldest to youngest . . . the morning's events hidden behind a façade of appropriate loving demeanor on freshly washed faces. Bits and pieces of the sermon . . . something about, burning in hell . . . God's ultimate wrath . . . the devil's trickery. When it's over, the children are dismissed to their respective Sunday school classes. The pastor asks Ruben to be the guest teacher in mine. He stands unprepared and nervous, hemming and hawing, struggling to find something meaningful to say. Looking down at The Bible in his hand as though seeing it for the first time, he thumbs through the pages, finds a passage and reads something about the sin of rage. Committing to it, he hangs his head in mock contrition like some over emoting B movie actor. My peers are quiet, riveted, focused as they wait for the rest of the story. Slowly, deliberately, he points a finger at me. "I almost lost my temper before coming here this morning because of that one right there! The devil plays tricks in my house. I had to call upon God to help me control my anger!"

Oh brother! Puzzled, quizzical, hot poker eyes bore through me. Why would you do that to such a nice man, they're asking. The handprint on my face burns like fire. Later that day, and for the first time, I rebel by hiding his precious brush under that hamper.

"Please make him keep his promise. Make him go away," I pray.

The effects of abuse may remain dormant until an adverse experience reopens old wounds from the past, further traumatizing the adult survivor (McQueen et al., 2009).

Fifteen

While her eyes were closed, mine were open to the possibilities of Angels walking among us. They walked onto my stage at the darkest hours. And they came in the Earth suits of Gram, first and second grade teachers, a seventh grade art teacher, and others. I recognized them because my world was so devoid of emotional sanity. If a kid could see the signs, how was it that Momma missed them? Because also crossing her path were common people exhibiting uncommon strength and valor. Those Angels presented tidings, a gift, a fork in the road, a choice, a message.

But she refused to listen. Momma's brother spirited her away to a secret location in another city. She stayed for six months—just long enough to begin developing self-esteem and self-respect on the way to a new life—a new life cut short by a knock at the door one evening. The stranger standing on the doorstep apologized for having the wrong address. One week later, the door is opened to Ruben—crying and pleading, snot running down his lip, promising never to hit, kick, or spit on her again . . . blah, blah, blah—bullshit, bullshit, bullshit! That stranger was the private investigator he'd hired to hunt her down and, unfortunately, obsessive stalking behavior equaled to love and caring in her book.

"He always came back to get me," she'd say. "The least I could do was give him another chance if he went through all that trouble. I just know it. This time will be different."

She borrowed money from many in her circle to get away from him, used the money, then returned to him, taking no responsibility for paying it back, and never acknowledging the people who'd given their support when she most needed it. The helping person became a persona non grata when she reunited with him, and was promptly banished from our lives as well. As she went through family and friends, there were fewer and fewer in her circle until there were none but us.

She made justifications to boomerang back and negotiated reality by putting blinders on. During the honeymoon phase, she and Ruben colluded to sacrifice either Aaron or me to stand in for her beatings. And when we complained, she kept us in line with guilt.

"Your Poppa is just stressed out from the pressure of making a living for this big ole' family. You should be happy that we at least have food to eat and a roof over our heads."

While he scapegoated Aaron and me, she used Jewel as hers; passive-aggressively blaming her for any little thing that went wrong in the house. Cunning and sneaky, she pretended to love all her children equally, pretended to be a good mother in front of strangers while focusing her hatred on Jewel behind closed doors. No one, and I mean, no one got out unscathed.

It was morning, but still dark when Momma shook me awake. "Come with me," she whispered urgently. Wiping the sleep from my eyes I stumbled after her to the baby's crib. Socorro's legs were red and welted with handprints and she was gasping and hiccupping, trying to cry soundlessly. Tears slid down the sides of her face. The pain on her face was torturous.

"Look at what he did to my baby," Momma exclaimed.

He'd actually spanked a six month old baby to the point of leaving angry red handprints on her legs. At that moment she transferred the memory to me so she could sleep the sleep of the oblivious. The two of them had a habit of awakening me from sleep because they needed a witness. Him at night by slapping me, her in the mornings to show me some awful thing he'd done to her or one of the children. I was so overcome I couldn't breathe and vomited every time I thought about baby Socorro. I had my first migraine that day, and was unable to eat or sleep for days afterward. Sometimes when my mind transports me to that very moment—every smell, every taste, every sight, and most of all, every feeling is still there. When she was about two, Momma attempted to show her how to smile by using her index fingers to push up the corners of her mouth.

"There, that's how you smile. Don't you know how to smile?" she'd repeat.

Not being able to smile told the outside world something was wrong. That simply couldn't happen. Neither saw anything wrong with a two-year-old baby who was unable to smile without it looking forced—no happiness behind the eyes because there was nothing to smile about. Eventually, she learned to fake it, the result of which is the loud cackling at Aaron's Memorial. She was still that little baby gasping for air, trying not to cry. But it's more complicated than that. Cackling with joy at our brother's Memorial, made her seem genuinely happy to have one less to compete with for the attentions of our parents. The constant scapegoating took away her ability to empathize with the victims.

Momma took advantage of her children's neediness with a manipulation I'll call learned helplessness. Complaining about some petty problem she's having with one of her adult children, usually one of her making, the pot gets stirred. Of course, it's all behind the target person's back.

"Oh, really? Hmmm." And then, I'll say something like, "Well, why don't you talk to her?"

And she'll say, "I have," when I know she hasn't.

Then, I'll say, "Well, what do you want me to do about it? I'm sure it's about something else all together. Leave me out of it."

The only way to stave off the coming scapegoating is brutal honesty. "Take the fall for me. Step into character for me," is what she is saying, but I dodge and sidestep because, in the end, it always turns out to be someone else's fault, never hers. It's Ruben's. It's one of the sister's. It's the weather. It's because she's retired. It's because she's old, and the list goes on. It's her way of deflecting reality because, otherwise, she'd have to acknowledge some very painful stuff. Not counting the verbal, psychological, psychic, and emotional abuse that went on all the time, in a good year, our mother suffered through many episodes of physical violence. Hypothetically speaking, let's say it was six times a year. That's one episode every two months . . . six beatings per year . . . times twenty years of marriage . . . equals a hundred and twenty instances of violence over the lifetime of their relationship. That is a lot of abuse for a person to endure, and a lot of abuse for children to watch. In reality, there were far more than a hundred and twenty episodes because domestic violence is not some static thing that happens once, and then, not again until the same time next month. And since abuse is actually about power and control, it escalates over time. When the victim falls into justification and denial, the more empowered the abuser becomes. And it is the abuser's whims, moods, circumstances, and triggers that govern the frequency of occurrence, not staying out of the way, not keeping our mouths shut, or any of the other things we were told to do to appease the tyrant. Domestic violence is completely unmanageable, yet the family's mission is to keep it secret, the polar opposite of what the family should do. Keeping violence secret entrenches the sickness, allowing it to spread and infect every member of the system. Frequently, Ruben got on these bents, brutally beating and holding her hostage for days on end, and then used sick days to keep his reign of terror from being interrupted by the minor detail of work. Appearances to the outside world never reflected the sheer terror and chaos behind closed doors. Aaron, Jewel, and I were debriefed and threatened each morning before school.

"Don't tell anyone what goes on inside this house. If I catch you talking to any of your little friends about this, I'll snap your necks like dried twigs." Or he'd say something like: "If I find out you've told anybody, I'll kill your Momma while you're gone and you'll come home to her lifeless body. Do you understand me? Do you hear me?"

"Yes," we answer in frightened unison . . . constant fear and chaos on one side . . . the burden of our mother's life or death on the other. We dared not tell. Momma bludgeoned us with our love for our siblings, told us we would be taken away from each other if we told. No outside intervention was allowed because they knew what they were doing was not normal, and keeping the secrets allowed him to continue the terror in private. After tiring of beating and terrorizing her, he went back to work like it was just another day, all happy and upbeat, leaving her looking like a swollen faced, black-eyed monster with welts and bruises all over its body. What could the children do but tiptoe on eggshells? What would set him off was unknown—where the landmines were buried, also unknown. Before walking out the door each morning, he confiscated her car keys, credit cards and money, unplugged the phone from the wall and took them when he left for the day. Everyone served the sentence until he decided she/we were captive no more. As the violence escalated toward her, it also escalated toward Aaron and me. Momma used selective blindness and learned helplessness to cope. Aaron, Jewel, and I had no choice but to either experience it, or stand by helplessly and watch it. Making it worse was the fact that our mother didn't seem to connect with our reality.

"I would be gone in a heartbeat if I caught him abusing my children," she'd said. "But since he loves you all, I'll continue to make the sacrifice."

Sixteen

Not for the reasons you might think, sneaking out of the house was a regular thing, no matter day or night. The violence is so frequent and alarming that I risk my life to save hers, proving that I am more concerned for her well-being than she is for mine.

Two city blocks stand between the pay phone and me. I am ninja, swift and covert, nimbly scaling six-foot rock walls with gymnastic aplomb, vaulting over lawn mowers and doghouses. Staying off the main streets is the only way to keep from getting picked up for breaking curfew. Capture would shift the focus from why I am desperately hiding in the bushes—the real reason I am alone in the dark, the real reason I am desperate to make a call from a payphone in the middle of the night. In a time when 911 and cell phones don't exist, I dial the number from memory—make the call anonymously—retrace my footsteps—and slip back into the house through the bedroom window as though I'd been there all along. Wringing with sweat and guilt, I pull the covers under my chin and wait for the doorbell to ring. When they leave, he is incensed that the cops keep showing up.

"Those nosy goddamned neighbors need to mind their own goddamned business," he fumes.

When the house is quiet, Aaron and I meet at the side yard near the trashcans. Once clear of the subdivision, we use flashlights to light the ground for the half-mile trek to the Annex. We climb over the chain link fence guarding the trampolines and jump and giggle to exhaustion. Then we sit in the cairn to howl—sending ululating, plaintive notes of pent up pain and rage wafting onto the night air far into the distance. Rumors about dangerous wolves escaped from a traveling carnival circulate the neighborhood. We watch Poncho Villa and the Cisco Kid, Tarzan and Cheetah, Buck Rodgers, and Lon Chaney. . . laughing until we can barely breathe. We can't look at each other without bursting into unending, uncontrollable waves of breathless giggles and crying.

"Wolves, you say? Yeah, those wolves escaped from a carnival all right," he gasps between fits of laughter.

We laugh so hard I'm afraid of passing out, or peeing my pants, until my abdominals feel as though they've done a thousand crunches. Just the thought of wolves in the desert is enough to make me burst into giggles in the middle of class, on the bus, or walking home alone. I can't help it. It's funny how gullible people can be. Eventually, the howling morphs into Tarzan yells and Cheetah screeches, and one-upping each other to see who can scream the loudest. Rumors change. Bigfoot is alive and well, smelling like death, living in a cave at the foot of the mountains, and hiding among the saguaros and tumbleweeds.

By the time Momma goes back to college to finish her bachelor degree, I'm fourteen. She says she's doing it to lift his heavy burden as sole provider for the family. She hopes this will stop him from being so violent. Yeah, and if he's only a little violent, then everything should be great going forward. She lays out her reasons, explains them over and over, as she tries to convince herself because there is no convincing me. It really doesn't matter why she thinks she's doing it. Finally doing something is what makes sense! She is finally making a decision. And hopefully, the byproduct will be an awakening. That's what matters.

Ruben views her absence as a personal affront. He is losing control. Guns multiply around the house. It's like they keep having babies just like Momma and Ruben. I find them stashed everywhere; the garage; the back of the linen closet under neatly folded sheets; the nightstand next to his side of the bed; his boot in the back of the walk-in closet; under his pillow; under the front seat of his car; wedged between the mattress and box springs. As a preemptive strike, I reconnoiter the perimeter every day to uncover the positions of old and new weapons. On one foray, in an old boot at the very back of the closet I uncover a little black case containing a syringe and vials of clear liquid labeled Winstrol. I've never heard of it, but I'm sure it's nothing good, so I wrap it back up and file the information for later. When the opportunity arises, I nonchalantly, ask Momma if Ruben has diabetes. "No! Of course not," is her indignant comeback.

"Why would you ask a question like that?"

"Oh, no reason. We were studying hereditary diseases in class today, that's all," I lie glibly.

There is no need to ask if he's a drug addict because she'll deny it. She doesn't want to know the truth.

Seventeen

There's still some heavy lifting to do the day after returning home from the Memorial. I kiss my husband goodbye and turn my attention to the mundane that is my life . . . load the dishwasher, put clothes in the washer, get Omar up for school. We talk and joke over breakfast—the start of a normal day. School is a block away. During the short walk, we talk some more. During my pregnancy, I took parenting classes and read child-rearing books. I learned how males are hard-wired for activity, and are more inclined to talk about feelings when engaged in physical activity . . . walking, shooting hoops, bike riding, and so on. This awareness has been quite helpful with both the males in my life. If I want to talk to Javier about something important, we take a bike ride, or go on a long nature walk. Walking Omar to school is a daily opportunity to find out what's important in his life. We also meet and greet neighbors . . . say hello to Audrey, the crossing guard in front of the school and engage in being part of the community, something strictly forbidden to me in my family of origin. While growing up I yearned to be part of a community. His childhood is so very different from the one I experienced, and I've worked hard to make that happen. He is taking his place in the community, so that he is not isolated the way I was. He has friends. The neighborhood kids show up at our home, and are welcomed. He participates in bike rides and hanging out at the park. He has sleep overs and birthday parties. I take them to the roller rink, or the ice rink, or the movies, or Trick or Treating. Yes, his childhood is a complete one hundred eighty from the one I experienced. His parents are involved and mellow and loving.

When I get back to the house, I can no longer postpone playing back messages. The first is from Officer Gomez of the East Los Angeles Highway Patrol. He's been assigned to the investigation.

"I guess I could have dealt with this sooner, but to be honest, I didn't have the emotional strength."

"Under the circumstances, that's understandable. First of all, let me express my deepest sympathies."

Kind words from a perfect stranger cause me well up with tears and break into tiny pieces. He waits patiently for me to gather myself. I switch outside my body.

He begins again. "I need to ask some questions. Would that be okay?"

"Yes."

The keyboard clicks in the background as he records my answers. In time, he asks if I have any questions for him.

"Do you know why he was walking across the freeway?"

"There are some homeless encampments under the overpass near where he died."

"How do you know he was homeless?"

"Before I took this job I worked with homeless men and women as an outreach liaison. We visited camps, disseminated literature about services, and in general, made contact to offer help. We also passed out trash bags like the one we found near his body. That's how we know he'd been in contact with an outreach worker. In his wallet we also found paperwork from a recent trip to the VA. Many homeless men are Veterans in need of mental health services. Did your brother have mental issues?"

"Yes," I answer. The next question screams to be asked, but I'm not sure I want to know the answer. Deep inhale. "Did he do it on purpose?"

"There's no evidence suggesting that ma'am. We believe he lived in one of the nearby camps. That's all."

Slow exhale.

"Do you know if he was coming or going?"

"No, we don't know that either." I can tell he's holding back. If he suspects Aaron did it on purpose, there's no concrete evidence. He's not going to deal in conjecture. Maybe he's trying to save me some anguish. I'm sure he's seen and heard it all before. We talk another fifteen minutes. Out of the blue, he confides the reason he is so compassionate for the homeless who are mentally ill.

"There was nothing you could have done. I have a fifteen year-old son who was diagnosed with bipolar disorder at ten. It's been a real struggle to keep him on his meds. You know as well as I do . . . when they turn eighteen, we have no control. I'm dreading that day," he ends quietly. A thoughtful silence bounces between us.

"I need to ask one more question," I begin cautiously.

"Did he suffer? I mean, afterwards?"

"Don't do this to yourself. The coroner determined he died instantly on impact. Thankfully, after all he'd been through, he didn't suffer like that."

Relief.

"Oh, by the way, one more question. On his California ID, the last name is spelled F-O-U-S-H-E-Z. Is that correct?"

I couldn't quite grasp what he was asking. Did they have the wrong person?

"No, it's spelled F-O-U-S-H-E-E, pronounced Fooshay."

"Oh, thanks. I'll clear that up."

"Excuse me. Are you sure you have the right person?"

"Yes. I'm so sorry. I didn't mean to get your hopes up."

"But how do you know?"

"His fingerprints."

"Oh."

"If you need anything else, don't hesitate to call. I'll mail a copy of the final report when I finish my investigation."

A 30-minute conversation sums it up. I sit staring into space. What did it mean? Foushez? Foushez? There was something familiar about it. What is it? FoushEZ. For Shee Z homey? My emotions meander from crying to laughing and back to crying again. Is it really meant to be a joke?

The next call I make goes to the Mortuary Society.

"Your brother's remains are ready. You still want them sent to the Dallas address, right?"

"Yes, that's right."

When Aaron and I were in our early twenties, he was preoccupied with death and dying. When you grow up the way we did, death is something you expect to happen sooner than later. Never know when you might take your last breath; may as well live it up. We were watching some stupid TV show when he made this statement.

"If anything happens to me, I don't want to rot in the ground and I sure as hell don't want to spend eternity in a box. Make sure that doesn't happen to me. Promise you'll take care of it, Leanne."

He wouldn't let it go until I promised.

"You don't need to worry about that. I'll take care of it. I promise."

And so it came to be. No one else in the family could handle it. Ruben couldn't. Momma couldn't. Our younger siblings couldn't. They'd all tried, but were unsuccessful, so I stepped in. It had been four days since his death. I was angry that his body was still in a refrigerated drawer because I offered my help from the beginning, but was turned down.

"We have it under control," is what Socorro said. When I take over, she does that insecurity thing she always does and tries to play little passive-aggressive games. Her interference is the reason no one else has gotten results. I stop engaging with her because she is a roadblock. I have to keep my promise.

The legally recognized next of kin is Aaron's adult son, James, who lives in Oklahoma. I need a signed release in order to get the body transferred to the crematorium. Their relationship was so complicated and fractured that it took four ten hour days of faxing paperwork back and forth before being able to wrangle the signature. During those four days, I slept very little. He was all alone in a drawer in the Coroner's office. When it is over, I am emotionally and physically drained.

Eighteen

After completing her BA and practice teaching assignment, Momma lands a job as a middle school English and Literature teacher. Keeping nothing for herself, on paydays she proudly endorses and hands over her paychecks to *him*. He's retired from the Army and works in the insurance industry. With only two more years to go before I am of age, I save money from a part-time job. My boss, Marietta, is recently divorced, beautiful, independent, and very different from my mother. At first glance, I admire her. She makes her own living, has freedom and autonomy—the very things I want from life. After working the job for two months, Momma hands the phone to me early one Saturday morning, tells me it's my boss. I'm not scheduled to work though.

"Tell Ruben I need a ride. My car won't start," she snaps. Her sense of entitlement makes me uneasy. In fact, she's downright nasty, but I dutifully relay the message. After all, they're the adults.

"You better keep your big-assed nose out of my fucking business you little cunt. I'm not giving that goddamned bitch a ride!"

Behind every corner, door, and window the elephant lurks. This time it steps into the open and lobs a grenade at my feet. The only thing to do is devise a plan to extricate myself from the situation as quietly, and as painlessly as possible. I tell no one of my intentions. He confronts me the same day I give notice at the old job.

"Why are you quitting your job?"

Checkmate! Feigning innocence, I give him the answers he wants to hear. "Oh, I found another one closer to home." Blah, blah, blah, bullshit, bullshit, bullshit. He knows nothing about me, doesn't see me, but I see him. I've seen him riding around with his girlfriends. I'm not surprised about that, but my boss? Really? What about not shitting where one eats or sleeps?

A month later, the acrid smell of impending disaster is in the air. He and Momma are sitting on the sofa engrossed in a deep, contentious conversation. He calls me over, orders me to sit down. Are they going to divorce? That would be wonderful! Please God! Make him go away! Make him go away! To my amazement, he starts to cry. The announcement: He's had many affairs with many women, including my previous boss, and the reason he's confessed is because Marietta threatened to tell Momma. He also confesses to using household money to wine and dine his conquests. And—Oh yeah, by the way, he's sorry. Prior to this revelation, Momma often said, "Your Poppa and I may have problems, but he's always been faithful. That's one thing I've never had to worry about."

Oh, please! Like no one ever saw that one coming! And what do they want from me? Why tell me? Wait for it. "I want you to help me talk your mother into forgiving me." They need a scapegoat to blame later. Why would I want to help them stay together? Hadn't they done enough already? From zero to sixty, an adult in a child's body from as far back as I can remember. I want to jump up and down and shout, "You idiots! Ass clowns! I don't give a damn whether you stay together, or not! Please, please let me live long enough to age out of this shit-hole!" Of course, when the dust settles, even with all the previous piles of crap before, and the many more to come, Momma finds her way to blindness and delusion.

The next day she confides that he'd confessed to having oral sex with his conquests, and that Marietta threatened him because he'd given her a venereal disease.

"I guess I'm gonna have to go to the doctor. How disgusting," she finishes.

This is by no means the first time she's over shared details of their sex life with me. Make it go away! Please, just make them go away!

On Saturday morning two weeks later, she's wearing that scared little girl mask when I leave for work. The latest honeymoon is over, and I won't be back until 4:00pm. She's on her own till then. After finishing my shift, Ruben orders me to take her car to pick up my sisters at his friend's house on the other side of town. This leaves her with no transportation. What he really wants is to get me out of the house. I do as I am told on the chance my sisters need me. Like an idiot, I drive round and round for an hour, mumbling the address under my breath—hesitating to call the house because I'm afraid to bother him, afraid of his wrath. I dial and redial the number. At first, there is no answer, but after about the tenth time, he picks up. Hoping he won't misconstrue my intent, I timidly ask if I have the right address. He gives another set of directions straight to the worst part of town. By now, it's dark. The freaks are out. Pimps and hoes know I'm out of place. They watch me drive round and round the block in the family station wagon, on a snipe hunt devised by my dear, caring father. My heart feels as though it's going to explode right out of my chest. Before the wheezing, uncontrollable shaking, crying and sweating hits, I manage to pull to the curb, open the door, hang my head out and vomit. When I pull myself together, I find a pay phone and call again. This time he gives the correct address. I pick up Socorro and Jewel from their babysitting job as quickly as I can, not sure I will make it back in time to save her. A trip that should have taken thirty minutes tops, has taken four hours. I pray I'm not too late.

On the drive, I can think of nothing but how he's recently taken to quietly sitting at the kitchen table in nothing but his bleached white skivvies unloading, cleaning, and reloading his guns. Behind his eyes emanates an inscrutable, cloistering darkness that blankets the house in fear. He lines up the bullets like little marching soldiers—always the same seven: six for the kids (the youngest hasn't been born yet), and one for Momma.

Anna and Arianne are locked out—banging on the front door trying to get in when I arrive. They were inside the house when I left to pick up Jewel and Socorro. I herd them into the car with the promise of an ice cream, then sneak into the house, grab a fistful of coins from the candy dish, and listen long enough to hear the familiar sounds of him beating her; her cries and pleas, his derision, the snap of the belt. Blood droplets trail up the plastic runner to the top of the staircase. From the corner DQ I make a phone call while my sisters try to decide between chocolate or vanilla. Trying to remain calm, I wait for the police cruiser to turn up the street.

"Did you call us? Do you live here," the officer asks.
"Yes."

He starts to give the same answer as usual. "I can't help. This is a domestic dispute." I pretend not to hear him, and proceed to unlock and push the front door open. The house is eerily dark except for a light from the kitchen exhaust fan spotlighting the blood trail on the stairs. The officers nervously cover their guns and order me out of the way.

"Police! Is anyone home? Does anyone need the police," he yells up the stairs. Silence. He turns to his partner. "No one's home."

He wants to wash his hands, but I press harder. "Yes, they are," I whisper. "I'm afraid for my mother! Please help us!"

He nods. A little louder this time, "Does anyone need the police?"

We wait. Disheveled and out of breath—huge perspiration stains under the arms of her torn, blood stained blouse—left eye swollen shut—Momma bolts down the stairs on the edge of hysteria, "Yes, I need the police. He has a gun! He has a gun!"

He lopes after her, cool as a breeze. One of the officers puts him in the cruiser without handcuffs; the other takes Momma aside and offers a short-term solution.

"I can keep him overnight, but that's about it, ma'am." She turns to me and asks, "What do you think I should do?"

"Ma'am, you can't leave this to your kid," he admonishes sharply.

"Momma, please make him go away," I beg in desperation.

"I just can't do that. He'll be all right tomorrow. You'll see."

"I see what you're up against. There's nothing I can do unless your mom presses charges."

He hands me a card, leans close enough so only I can hear.

"You can call me if things get too bad."

They take Ruben away. I take Momma to the ER. Hours pass. Around midnight, we walk through the door, and there he is leaning against the kitchen counter—arms folded—composed—pathologically calm—frightening. The hair stands up on the back of my neck. My heart almost jumps from my chest.

Before she's completely healed, he does it again. This time he beats her to a bloody pulp with his fists. He does his dirty work then leaves the house for days. It's all very calculated because he wants an excuse to stay with one of his girlfriends. On the way out the door, he stops long enough to slap me around, bloodying my nose. I stuff a tissue up my nostril, and for the second time in the same month, I pour my mother into the car and take her to the ER. The doctors and nurses minister to her . . . x-ray her face . . . check for internal injuries. The same doctor from last time examines swabs, cleans, and gently packs my nose.

"How did this happen," he asks kindly.

"He slapped me."

"Who?"

"My father," I say expecting the usual comeback.

Well, what did you do to deserve it? To my surprise, he proffers understanding.

"If you remember nothing from tonight, I want you to remember what I am about to say. Only cowards beat up women and children. You didn't do anything wrong! It's not your fault. Do you understand?"

I nod slowly. When he's finished with my nose, closing the curtain behind him, he walks away and leaves me sitting on the edge of the bed. Down the hall, a heated conversation ensues between the Dr. and his CO.

"Two times in the same month; someone has got to do something!"

The CO orders the young doctor to mind his own business. If not for the doctor's honesty, I wouldn't have been able to make another cognitive leap soon thereafter. In English the required reading is The Prince by Machiavelli. I read it concurrently with a series of autobiographies I find on his dresser about some semi-famous pimp turned author. Somewhere in the middle of a stream of consciousness, the two worlds meet. They rule their kingdoms using tactics of manipulation and strong-armed robbery of the soul. The Pimp's written account of psychological and emotional abuse and terror against women is a blueprint for the way the business of violence is conducted in my family. The Pimp is sadistic, narcissistic, sociopathic—isolating his victims, deriving pleasure from seeing, tasting, and feeling his victim's terror . . . murdering souls and crushing humanity. Ruben's face and The Pimp's are one in the same! There is little difference between the two.

Primed from an abusive childhood, Momma is the walking wounded; sticking around to prove that love really does conquer all. No matter how unworthy he proves to be, she hangs onto him, bows at the feet of The Prince to appease him, plugs her finger into the socket while praying for the day he will see her worthiness. And like the women in The Pimp's stable, she is the perfect victim, the perfect compliment, the perfect accomplice. He is brutal. She is checked out, numb, aloof, emotionless. They fit together like pieces of a puzzle. They dance together—whirling—dipping—spinning.

But I don't want to dance anymore. I don't want lies. I don't want darkness. I don't want to be a princess. I want truth, light, and education. I do not want to be taken care of at any cost. I will not prostitute my children's futures to remain a perpetual princess as my mother has. I will be queen.

She angrily confronts Socorro and Jewel for taking me away from the house when she most needed protection.

"You don't need to be working. Keep your asses at home so Leanne won't have leave me alone with him! And Leanne, you should to be here when I need help, not gallivanting around. You need to quit your job, too!"

Yep. That's what she said. As a result, I kept my job, but she made it a living hell every time I had to leave.

Nineteen

Late June – 1972

    Early weekday mornings, Aaron, Jewel, and I walk six blocks to the Y for swimming lessons. After lessons are done, our treat is staying until noon. Floating on my back in over chlorinated, eye stinging water, diamond facets peak and lap at the pool's edge . . . the sounds of life muffled under water. He runs . . . time slows . . . he leaps . . . contracts . . . time speeds up . . . "Cannon ball," Aaron yells right before the percussion blast and shower of liquid shrapnel. The waves rock my floating body from one end of the pool to the other.

    Ruben gathers us around the kitchen table to lay out summer vacation plans; a road-trip from El Paso to Gram's in Sand Springs. The ground rules: Don't embarrass him, do as he says, and keep your mouths shut! I want to see Gram, but I'm torn because the trip means concentrated time cooped up in a car with him. In Oklahoma he morphs into an affable, fun, and happy guy around his aunts, uncles, cousins, and family friends . . . someone they all love. That person is a complete stranger to us. We spend very little time with Gram. In an attempt to keep peace, from sun up to sun down, we haplessly shuttle from one relative's home to another. At dark, fall into bed one moment, only to be awakened by derisive early morning revelry. The pace is frenetic and exhausting. Gram politely refuses to visit her late husband's relatives living only a few minutes away in the next small town. This summer I find out why.

Grandfather Andre had eight siblings—three brothers, five sisters. Three of those sisters never stopped blaming Gram for his death. Ruben confirms that his aunts hate his mother. "They tore her clothes off right in front of us at my dad's funeral. They said she drove him away, said she poisoned him. She doesn't come with us because she just can't let bygones be bygones!" The admission is supposed to put the issue to rest, but it has the opposite effect on me. Who we are now began a long time ago, long before my parents were born, long before me. I want to know more. The only person I can ask is Gram's first cousin, Minnie. She'll know, and she'll tell me. Minnie's father, George, and Gram's mother, Dora, were siblings. Dora couldn't rake care of her children because she suffered from "nerves". As a result, she was committed to a mental institution and her children were separated and sent to live with relatives. Gram ended up with her uncle George. That's why she and Minnie were more like sisters than cousins. On the one day I am allowed to be with them, I ask the question: "Is it true they beat you up and ripped your clothes off, Gram?"

A look filled with meaning passes between the two women. Minnie does the talking.

"Truth is, they were mean people who needed someone to blame. They chose your Gram, even though what they accused her of was impossible. Before he died, Andre abandoned his family to live in Kansas City with one of his whores. That last year of his life, your Gram had no idea where he was. But they blamed her anyway. It wasn't her fault. You know what I say? He was a product of that crazy-assed family and there was something wrong with every last one of them, especially the boys! Andre's father, Markus was a son-of-a-bitch, shuckin' and jivin' in public while beating his wife and kids behind closed doors. The whole town knew. Andre's brother, Merikus, left home when he was just fourteen, and never stepped foot inside that house again. Markus and Merikus passed each other on the street like perfect strangers without so much as a nod of acknowledgement. They had such bad blood; Merikus didn't even come to his father's funeral. That should tell you something. We watched Andre kill his pain by drinking himself into a stupor most nights. It got so bad he couldn't keep a job and, and if he had stayed here any longer, he would have died sooner. Drinking himself to death was slower than jumping off a bridge. It was only a matter of time. One day, he up and disappeared leaving your Gram heartbroken. The next time we heard anything, he'd been killed in a bar room fight."

Gram leans forward, takes my hands in hers. With tears in her eyes, she whispers. "Do better baby. Do better. Climb up on the backs of your people. Learn to do better."

Late July -1972

Ruben leaves for New Mexico to check himself into a monastery for what is supposed to be a two-week stay. She sobs uncontrollably. All I can think is, "that's what he says." I don't believe a word of it. More than likely he's on a cocaine bender with his latest girlfriend.

"He needs to find God so he can kick his cocaine habit," she repeats between crying fits.

Four days later, he's back proclaiming to be healed! He becomes more and more agitated and erratic. She calls his boss and tells him about their problems. The boss orders him to see a psychiatrist. While sitting at the kitchen table for yet another of those tense breakfasts, he makes a chilling proclamation.

"My psychiatrist thinks this family is my problem!"

He takes Momma hostage, accuses her of having affairs, and then beats her for denying it and for calling his boss. Mercifully, the siege ends five days later with him going back to work, but not before threatening to kill her if she leaves the house for any reason. That means no hospital, no grocery shopping, no nothing—just fear and imprisonment. He takes the phone. And to further make his point, he creeps into the house when least expected. All of the sudden, there he is, standing in the kitchen, calmly leaning against the counter with that wild look in his eyes. Paranoid of every little noise, I am hyper vigilant—imagining him dressed in head to toe black—grease paint smeared all over his face—skulking in like a leopard with spring loaded muscles—ready to pounce—a killing knife clenched between his teeth—blending into the shadows—laying in wait. One by one, as we cross the kill zone, he deftly slits our throats, piles the bodies up like garbage, and disappears us to the desert for the buzzards.

Days pass; unpredictability gives way to predictable noontime visits. I help her devise a plan of action. We sneak away to the Teacher's Credit Union to apply for a loan. In the state of Texas, a married woman can't get a loan without her husband's signature, even if it is the credit union associated with her job. After filling out the application, the loan officer (I'll call her Mrs. Peña) invites us to sit for an interview. Momma hides behind dark sunglasses.

"Take your glasses off Momma. Let her see." Reluctantly, she slides them away from eyes buried in shiny, black rings so dark it looks as though they are painted on with a marker . . . shocking enough to elicit an audible gasp from Mrs. Peña. I passionately plead our case. When I'm finished, Mrs. Peña speaks slowly and deliberately to me . . . face-to-face, as though Momma's not there, never breaking eye contact . . . never blinking.

"All I need is the signature. When your mom brings this back, she can have the money."

We walk out of the office with her whining all the way across the parking lot, her voice louder and more hysterical with each step.

"I can't get him to sign this! He won't! There is no getting away from him!"

I say nothing until we are safely ensconced inside the car away from prying ears.

"Momma, she meant for me to sign it," I answer peevishly.

After practicing on a piece of paper for a couple of minutes, I forge his signature.

"Come on Momma, we're gonna go get that money!"

Packing takes place haphazardly. Once the car is packed, she refuses to leave! I am astonished, utterly gob smacked. Why? She wants to talk to his psychiatrist. Rummaging among his things, she finds the card.

"Momma, he's not seeing a psychiatrist, and you know it! Please, let's just go! What if the psychiatrist tells him you called? Then what? I'm scared! Please let's not be here when he gets back!"

Dr. Durbin returns her call after a heart-pounding hour. He told Momma that Ruben planned to kill us, and that she should take her children and leave, and that he had not been to any of his appointments. Instead of taking that information and making a break for it, she rips the Dr. to shreds with displaced rage, blames him for putting her life in danger! Ruben's threatened to kill her so many times. Does she forget, or does she just not believe? Every time he beats her, he toys with the idea of killing her right in front of us. He's always been scary. Why is this time any different? If I had asked, I don't think she could have formed a cogent answer.

In the month leading up to this moment, my mission had been to steal his ammo and discard it in the neighbor's garbage can under the rotting banana peels and coffee grounds. No matter how much I take, the stockpiles continue to multiply. I can't keep up. I walk around with a churning stomach and a psychic tingling at the base of my neck that won't go away. One night, I bolt upright from a nightmare in which a nondescript monster is chasing me. It stays just out of my range of vision so I can never see what or who it is. The smell of ozone is crisp and strong, and sickeningly sweet. I climb out the bedroom window to his car at the curb and steal the ammo clip from the Luger under the driver's seat. The following day, he takes her for a drive to a remote place in the desert, takes out the gun, puts it to her head, and pulls the trigger. Unsuccessful at blowing her brains out, he pistol whips her, accuses her of stealing his shit, and chokes her into unconsciousness.

When she comes to, he chokes her until she passes out again and again. By the time the car pulls into the driveway they've been gone half the day. I am frantic. She's wearing that scared little girl face. Bruises ring her neck. When we are alone, she recounts her harrowing ordeal.

"Why would anyone mess with his stuff, especially his guns?" she asks. "I kept telling him, nobody would do that!"

I can't believe what I'm hearing. I want to say, "Really Momma, really? Why would anybody do that? You're not dead, are you? He didn't blow your brains out the side of your skull, did he?" Why she needed to confirm that the danger is real is beyond me. Clearly, he's out of control and getting worse! All it would take is one wrongly placed blow. All it would take is for the gun to be loaded the next time. All it would take is for him to squeeze her neck a little too long. And what about us? Don't we count for anything? Why would anybody mess with his stuff? That question is not the one that needs to be asked. The answer was clear . . . indisputable . . . unequivocal . . . absolute. The question that needed to be asked was: Why am I still here?

Early August - 1972

She is a timid, inexperienced driver having only had a driver license for a year and a half. So I drive, without sleep, all the way from El Paso to Carson City, Nevada where her sister Leslie lives with her husband Rob and their two children. I attempted to get her to go someplace a little less obvious, someplace where he can't easily track us down, someplace like Arizona, or New Mexico where we know no one. If she applied for welfare, we could make it until finding jobs, but when I mention the prospect of her working, she flat out refuses to take it under advisement.

"No one in this family has ever been on welfare, and never will be," she says with pride and anger.

The day after arriving in Carson City, I land a job at a printing company that pays well enough to rent a decent enough place for all of us. Leslie and Rob become a variable I had not counted on. They talk her into seeking God at their Apoxolic Faith church camp in Portland. So going to camp becomes more important than finding a job, a place to live, or conserving our meager resources. I beg for rational pragmatism.

"Doesn't it say somewhere in the Bible that God only helps those who help themselves?" I counter. "We need to save our money. You need to find a job so we can afford a place of our own. That way, we won't have to go back. He's going to blame me for helping you, and you know he's going to beat me for it."

She can't see, or doesn't seem to care that if we travel down this road again, we will soon be back in the eye of the maelstrom. She is orchestrating the fall, and I am pissed at the betrayal. They label me rebellious—the devil's plaything in need of a good "Jesus butt whooppin'". The ones in adult bodies win the argument. Leslie and Rob convince her that God is the only solution. With the brain washing complete, and the betrayal set in motion, she tells me to add my paycheck to the pot. Otherwise, we won't have enough money. Trading one devil for another, we travel to Portland.

While conducting in-depth interviews of battered women, McGee (2000) found that male abusers exhibit several common psychological and emotional antecedent abuse behaviors as build up to physical abuse—triggers like money, disagreeing with the man, accusing the woman of infidelity, crying children, religiosity, a woman's attempt to leave the relationship, anything that goes wrong in his life. Children of these unions are likely not only to suffer physical abuse, but also emotional abuse such as witnessing the abuse of their mothers, humiliation, blatant preferential treatment of other children in front of the abused child, deprivation of sleep and play time, killing the child's pet, threatening to kill the pet, and mistreating the pet.

Twenty

Apoxolic Faith church services are otherworldly—what with people flopping around on the floor like fish out of water, writhing bug-eyed and poker-faced, gasping for air, crawling, screaming, crying, speaking in tongues, and frothing at the mouth. One of the Sisters circulates the crowd with a stack of white cloths throwing them over the legs of women whose "Little House on the Prairie" dresses have ridden up immodestly while worshipping/rolling on the floor. On the microphone the minister flagellates the backs of the believers with tuneless singsong phrases.

"All ye children, all ye children. Be not afraid. Drown in his blood. Speak to your Lord. Call on him. He will listen. Do not be afraid."

The congregation is lost in a world of fervent worship. After three hours, the minister emits a wolf call, the purpose of which is to calm the fervor and bring the faithful to order. As if in the last throes of orgasmic pleasure they quiet. One last howl turns them into respectable pod people just in time for bed. The camp consists of twenty small cabins crowded with beds. Women and girls wear modest dresses with flour sack patterns of pink and blue flowers, or gingham checks . . . the length hovering just above the ankles. Aunt Leslie tells Momma that I have to straighten my Afro to fit in, and when I refuse, Momma tells me she is embarrassed that I exist, calls me names, berates me. It's like they're attempting to force me to my knees to pray. I refuse. Aunt Leslie tells me I've got the devil in me and that I need to release myself to the Lord. Forcing a person to take on your religion is just plain wrong. Again, I refuse.

That first night, we are immediately ushered into a service. Aaron, Jewel, and I sit together. When it is time to get on our knees and speak in tongues, we kneel side-by-side unsure of what to do. Next to us, a woman screams and starts speaking in tongues, and we spend the next hour developing hernias, snorting and giggling as silently as we can, trying not to break up laughing. One of the main rules we learn the next day are: Males on one side of the aisle; females on the other, even opposite sex siblings are discouraged from talking to each other. The only time I get to see Aaron is during worship. At the beginning of week two, I plan a clandestine ditch of the three-hour morning service by palming a note to him. When the faithful are busy rolling around on the floor, we sneak out to smoke a joint. He ducks into the men's restroom, tells me he'll be right back. I hide behind a cabin to keep from being discovered. If we're caught, the penalty will be swift and religious. One of the faithful, I'll call Dan, goes into the same restroom a few seconds later. When Aaron doesn't come out right away, I get a funny feeling. This time the ozone smell is bitter and putrid. It's taking too long! I run into the men's room.

"Aaron! Where are you," I yell. In the corner, Dan's hand is on my brother's crotch. It takes a few stunned moments before I can wrap my mind around what I'm seeing.

"What are you doing," I screech loudly. "What are you doing to my brother, you fucking pervert? I'm telling Momma, you piece of shit motherfucker!"

As I lunge, Aaron grabs me, pins my arms at my sides, picks me up and carries me out the door. An 8-foot chain link fence surrounds the campgrounds. Normally, our fence-climbing prowess would make short work of it, but the razor wire coiled at the top presents an impassable obstacle. We are captives once again. We pace the fence line like caged circus tigers before admitting that the only way out is the way we came in. And now, it is a matter of the devil you know versus the one you don't. Aaron says he'd rather be beaten by Ruben than have to deal with a Cult full of perverts.

"Talk to Momma. Tell her I want to go home. Tell her it's because of Dan. Tell her what you saw."

"You know she won't listen to me Aaron!"

"Just try for me," he pleads.

"I'll do my best," I promise reluctantly. Here's how that conversation went.

"I saw Dan molesting Aaron in the restroom! He had him cornered by the sinks when I came in."

"What were you doing in the men's room?"

"I was waiting for Aaron to come out and when he didn't, I went in to see if he was all right."

"How dare you lie about something like that," she screams.

"I'm not lying! I saw him! Ask Aaron! He'll tell you!"

"These are church going men," she extols. "They would never do anything like that!"

"I saw it with my own eyes! Please listen to me for once! I'm not lying! Ask Aaron! He wants to go home!"

"You're lying, and if you keep it up, I'll knock your teeth down your throat," she returns with seething anger.

"Why would I lie about that? I'm not a liar! You are," I yell hoarsely. "You make up stories to cover for that crazy man you're married to! You tell me to lie when you have black eyes and can't go to work! You tell me to lie when your friend Katie calls to see how you're doing. I lie for you every day of my life! You want to know what I've learned? A lie is better than the truth! Don't put the blame me if you want to go back to him! You didn't even try to get a job! You didn't even try to take care of us! I'm the one who takes care of you, and I'm sick of it!"

"You don't take care of me. Why would you say something like that?"

"I drove you to the hospital when I didn't even have a permit! I take you to the hospital every time he beats you so badly you can't move without me helping you to the bathroom!"

I'm so angry, spit is flying from my lips, and I am crying, and hyperventilating. The following evening Aaron and I are reprimanded and humiliated in front of the congregation for skipping services. She sits passively, giving her allegiance to new perpetrators as we are labeled devil worshipers, sinners, and incorrigibles. She takes the perpetrators side once again.

Ruben is waiting when we get back to Carson City. Aaron goes home with the devil he knows, and Momma blames me for telling him where we are.

"Why would I do that? I don't want to live in the same house with your crazy, violent husband. You know he's going to blame me for you leaving him, and you know it! You're both setting me up!"

She says nothing, but I can see her giving in. She wants to go back. I have no job. Our money has been spent on Cult encampment. A few days later, we pack the car just in time for school to start. I am seething; so incensed. I don't say two words on the drive back. She, on the other hand, keeps explaining why she needs to do this. I tune her out and drive. We stop for food at the halfway point. I hand her the keys and tell her I'm tired. She drives for about thirty minutes before stopping, saying she's too tired to continue, and pushes the keys at me. I let them fall to the ground.

"I will never help you again!"

I get into the passenger side without a word. She complains how tired she is the whole trip.

The old patterns return. He takes his anger out on Aaron and me. "Why do you let him treat us like this," I ask because now, I sugar coat nothing. I call her out at every opportunity.

"Just kill him with kindness," she replies.

"What is that supposed mean? I'm not blind like you. He hates us!"

"Where would you get an idea like that? Your Poppa doesn't hate us. He's just a very complicated man."

"That's a ridiculous lie and you know it!"

Early September 1972

He makes the family dog disappear to punish me. His name was Ruffo. I was his human, the one with whom he had that special bond. I fed, watered, brushed, walked, and cared for him. He was the sweetest being. He'd been kicked across the room enough times to know when to flee. Like the rest of us, he knew when to steer clear of the chaos, but he was ten, getting older, not as spry, and less able to nimbly dive under furniture when the bombs exploded. After Ruben got back from Vietnam, Ruffo was frightened of him. He did weird things like sitting in his closet barking and growling at his shoes for what seemed no reason, but Ruffo was tuned into something. He had a sixth sense, and so did I. This particular time we were locked down on a hostage siege lasting three or four days. Acting as though every thing was normal, the kids go to and from school each day. I pick up Anna and Arianne at school.

Back at the house, Ruffo failed to come to the door to greet me, as was his normal routine. Momma wears that little girl look. Ruben glowers at everyone, especially me. I attempt to keep some normalcy. While they sit at the table eating the after school snacks I've prepared, I start dinner—cutting up potatoes, carrots, celery, onions, and a chicken, dump it all in a Dutch-oven with water, salt and pepper, and shove it inside the oven to bake for two hours at 350 degrees. After that's done, I go out to the back yard just in case Ruffo's been locked outside all day and needs water. He's not there. I comb the neighborhood frantically calling his name. It begins to dawn on me with certainty that he is not coming back. I can't tell you why I knew it, but I knew he was gone for good. There is a heavy pall in the house. My heart aches. Ruben's done something to him. I just know it. When the dinner dishes are done, he orders me to take the kitchen trash to the can outside. My hand grips the lid. I hesitate—open it—peer in. The moment is surreal. Partially covered in cigarette butts, coffee grinds, and other household garbage is what looks like a large, matted stuffed toy. Its tongue lolls to one side, hanging between the teeth of its partially open mouth. Its eyes are open and glazed milky white. With his life force gone, he is smaller than when alive. Trying to figure out whether I can trust my eyes, whether my brain is working right, I am intent in the moment. He sniggers sinisterly behind me (he, he, he) causing a flight or fight response. Startled, I twirl around to face him. My skin snaps tightly around my scalp, every muscle at the ready, my heart skips a beat as I fight blind panic.

"He was a worthless piece of shit anyway," he says calmly. "The next time you help your Momma leave me, that will be you."

He did it on purpose! He did it to punish me! He killed him! He killed my pet! With a gloating smile, he turns slowly and coolly and walks away victorious. I close the lid. Holding my mouth with a hand, I race to a far corner of the yard and vomit until nothing is left. My heart hurts.

The next day is trash day. After the can is dumped into the belly of the garbage truck, it is as though Ruffo never existed. At the end of the driveway, flies cover a coagulating brownish blob that leaked from the bottom of the can while it sat at the curb. With a look of satisfaction and smugness, Ruben orders me to hose it away. I escape to watch my body find the high-pressure nozzle, numbly screw it onto the hose, and robotically sweep the water from side to side. It wasn't as though they sat me down and said, "These are the rules! Don't talk about this. Don't mention it. Don't ask. It's over!" I just knew. But this time, I rebel by catching Momma in an unguarded moment a week later.

"Tell me what happened to Ruffo. I deserve to know!"

"Oh, he was old. He probably went to the desert to die."

I stand face to face with her, looking directly into her eyes.

"That's a lie," I counter quietly. "Ruben killed him. Please stop covering for him."

A quivering bottom lip betrays her. She looks away.

"He'll kill us all if you don't keep your mouth shut," she whispers.

"Don't you get it? It doesn't matter if I keep my mouth shut, or not. He's going to kill us anyway. If he can do that to Ruffo, he'll do it to us!"

As if killing Ruffo wasn't enough, a couple of weeks into my senior year he beats the crap out of me on a Friday. It's the worst beating I've experienced to date . . . lasting so long he took a fifteen minute rest . . . sitting on the edge of the bed clutching the belt, puffing and wheezing long enough for me to imagine him keeling over writhing in pain while holding his chest. When rested, he jumps up, grabs my wrist, digs his thumb into the middle of my palm, and twists my arm up and back so my palm faces skyward. I have to bend from the waist to keep him from breaking my arm. He stripes my back with long angry crisscrosses. The more I cry and plead for him to stop, the more frenzied he becomes.

"Stop crying! If you cry, it's going to get worse for you! That doesn't hurt! I'm the one who's hurting right now! I'm the only person in the world that could possibly love you and you disgust me. I cry a tear for you every goddamned day. You will never learn a thing! You're a stupid little cunt, just like your mother. Why can't you just do what I tell you, you worthless little piece of shit?"

He stops whipping long enough to grab the front of my shirt and pull me nose to nose. Spit mists my face, leaving behind the green gas stench of the bacteria decaying one of his molars. He lets go, grabs fistfuls of my hair and violently shakes my head back and forth, ripping out clumps from the root. "You look at me when I'm talking to you," he snarls through clenched teeth. His hands close around my throat. I can't breathe. I claw and fight. My eyes feel as though they are going to pop out of their sockets. Before the darkness sets in, my last thoughts are—"Just let go. It'll be over soon." I feel my body sliding to the ground.

Radiant light pours through slatted blinds. Floating like snowflakes, fine dust particles dance between daggers of light. From the porch of an old farmhouse, I stare into the distance. Wind chimes tinkle. Every blade of grass, every tree, the sun, and the moon exudes infinite love. A woman stands next to me. We stare into the distance focused on the swiftly moving dark clouds.

"You have to go back," she whispers.

"Why? There's nothing left for me. Please don't send me away."

Ominous clouds gather in puffy, dark, roiling confusion. The storm is here. She takes my hand and tells me to count backwards from a hundred. 100, 99, 98, 97, . . . I awake to my face being slapped back and forth.

"Get your ass up from there. Stop faking. I'm not through with you yet! The next time you help your Momma leave me, I will kill you! Do you hear me? From here on out, you'd better stay out of my fucking business! You understand me?"

The last slap sends my head glancing off the sharp corner of the dresser. I drag unsteadily to my feet.

The person in the mirror is unrecognizable—puffy, swollen scared little girl eyes, fingerprint bruises ringing her neck, cheeks bloated double their normal size. Every muscle aches. Clothing aggravates the welts on my back—excruciating. In the following days both eyes turn black, then deep purple. In time the purple fades to dark brown, then yellow half moons that take months to fade completely. But by Sunday the eyes are a black so salient, no amount of makeup will hide them. I don't recognize my face in the mirror. I wonder if I ever will, if I will ever look normal again.

He feigns remorse—is overly nice—slathers butter on his tongue—fucks with my head. In his mind it is over.

"You won't remember this years from now," he repeats. "Dogs and kids don't remember the past. You'll come to forgive your dear old Poppa one day. You know I love you, sugar pie, don't you?"

I want to say, "No, I don't!"

"I'm a good father," he continues. "Just don't want you to go astray, so I have to spank you because that's how I show my love. What do you think would happen if I weren't here to turn your dumb ass around? You just need to stop doing things to make me mad. Stop doing things to spite me."

On cue: "Yes Poppa. You're right, Poppa. I'm sorry Poppa. I won't do it again. I'm sorry I hurt you. I didn't mean to."

Lying little android, taking the blame, carrying the shame. He batters me, knocks me to the ground for minor infractions, mostly, just because I'm handy. He throws me around like a rag doll, as disposable as garbage. I'm afraid of him and venture to tell the truth on three occasions while living under his roof. After the words leave my mouth, I brace for the beat down, but his reaction is an odd, high-pitched, plaintive voice filled with hurt.

"Why? Why, would you be afraid of me, sugar pie? You shouldn't be afraid of me. Strangers are the ones you should fear. Not me. You're wrong to be afraid of me. You're wrong to feel that way."

Deftly, expertly, he twists it; making himself the long-suffering sympathetic, heroic character and me, the ungrateful, uncaring, unfeeling degenerate. "You'll understand when you have children. This is what it's like in the real world. You should fear strangers, not me," he finishes. Really? If this is the 'real world', how was I supposed to navigate outside the confines of this convoluted family dynamic? How was I going to be able to trust? And why was it my responsibility to make it okay for him to be violent? From my standpoint, strangers were not the ones I needed to fear. With my soul separated from my body, I go to school on Monday. Everyone stares. Only a brave few dare ask, "What happened?"

"Oh, I fell," I lie. At lunch, waiting in line for the pay phone, the events of the past months churn in my gut. I pick up the receiver. The bell rings. Shuffling to class with hundreds of eyes crawling all over my back, I hear them whispering.

"I wonder what she did to deserve it."

I sit in class daydreaming violent scenarios in which, I kill him again and again. Nervous twitters infiltrate.

"You need to go to the principal's office," Mrs. Abel repeats impatiently.

Two officers—I recognize the one who yelled at Momma for trying to get me to decide for her, the one who gave me his card. I tell him about the beating. He studies my face, never taking his eyes off mine.

"Did he do this?"

"Yes."

"Why are you wearing a turtleneck? It's 95 degrees!"

I scoot the sleeves up to show the angry red stripes covering my arms. I turn down the turtleneck to reveal the bruising around my neck.

His car is in the driveway. The only time he is at the house this early in the day is during a hostage siege. I take a deep breath, open the door. Sitting at the kitchen table is the enemy.

"Sit down," he gestures quietly. "The police were here threatening me. Why would you embarrass me like that?"

"I didn't do it to embarrass you."

"If not to embarrass me, then why would you do something like that?"

"Because I'm scared of you."

"But, why would you be afraid of me? I'm not some monster. I'm you're father! Do you really feel that way?"

"Yes," I answer with dead affect.

"You don't really think I'm a monster. Do you? I haven't really hurt you. With all my Special Forces training, if I really wanted to, I could've killed you by snapping your neck, but I didn't. The only reason you're still here is because I didn't want that!"

"Am I supposed to be grateful you didn't kill me?"

"You've got nothing to complain about and you've got no reason to be afraid of me. You know you did the wrong thing by calling the police, don't you? They threatened me! Do you want your sisters and brother put in a foster home because of your stupidity? If you ever embarrass me like that again, you know I'll have to kill you, don't you?"

He reaches across the table with lightening precision and slaps me off the chair. Standing up slowly and deliberately, I lock eyes with his. "I hate you!"

"Wh—wh—what did you say?"

"I said—I hate you."

"If I died tomorrow you'd regret it. That was the last thing I ever said to my dad. Now, let's try it again. You don't really hate your dear old Poppa, now do you?"

"Go ahead. Kill me. I'm not going to lie."

Blood dribbles unbidden from my nose down the front of my sweater and onto the floor. One drop. Two drops. Three. Four. Five. Usually, I look down at my feet, but this time I hold my head high. He is quiet. Six.

"Clean that mess up," he commands.

In a long unhurried motion, I drag my forearm across my nose smearing a long streak onto my sleeve.

"Clean it up," he orders more insistently this time.

"Or what? You'll beat me for bleeding?"

He blinks, stares at me for a long moment before turning on his heel and walking out the front door. He gets into his car, and drives away in a huff. When he is gone, Momma appears.

"If you ever talk to your father like that again, I'll knock your teeth down your throat."

One week later, my seventeenth birthday passes without fanfare. The rest of the seniors take cap and gown pictures. Not me. I am ashamed because I have two black eyes. There was nothing about my high school years I really wanted captured for posterity. And Proms were only fairy tales—no such thing as a Prince and Princess living happily ever after. No such thing.

Years later, when I relate this experience to my therapist, he is appalled.

"Today, your father would have been arrested and convicted for domestic violence, making terroristic threats, and child abuse. You and your siblings would have been removed from the home immediately and rightfully so. And if your mother escaped being arrested along with him, she wouldn't have been able to get you back until she got her shit together!"

A study conducted by Lisak & Beszterczey (2004) about the cycle of violence among death row inmates, found that three-quarters of the sample population had been scapegoated as a part of the process of childhood abuse. McGee (2000) also found that children's relationships with both parents and extended family were greatly affected by the strain of keeping the family secret of violence and not being allowed to have contact with friends or extended family.

Twenty One

Told in disjointed vignettes, family history turned out to be vital information that slipped out in anger. I listened, digested, and analyzed what I was told to forget. Only after Aaron's death was I able to completely break the code. His favorite stories from his childhood were about pouring kerosene on stray cats, and setting them on fire.

"They ran like little balls of fire with flames licking at their asses, screaming and crying like babies—fireworks on the 4th of July. Whoo wee!"

"Were they still alive, Poppa," I'd ask in disbelief and horror. "You mean, they were really alive?"

"Why do you keep asking that question, you damn dummy? A dead cat can't run, can it now? It's dead! Don't you get it? They were worthless pieces of shit that didn't matter to nobody. Why do you care so much? Let it go and stop asking questions."

Momma sat listening to the same stories, but seemed unable to put two and two together. To hurt little animals, or people, and then brag about it was downright criminal. And no matter how stupid he said I was, or how many times he called me a dummy, there had to be something wrong with anyone who did that to innocent animals. This type of behavior is a precursor in the development of serial killers. I often wondered whom he really was in the darkest recesses of his mind and if he could cross that line. He was so evil, I was certain there was a darker side to him than the one we saw. He was infinitely successful at drawing women into his lair. Not to excuse his behavior, I believe it was up to the women, the mothers, the grandmothers, and the aunts not to be so desperate for a man and to make better choices. Choosing better mates meant better fathers for their children. Choosing better fathers for their children meant well-adjusted adults who would, in turn, rear well-adjusted children. The women were the ones with the power to break the cycle. And they were the ones who needed to stop becoming accomplices to the walled-off, unreachable, and cruel, damaged men they kept choosing.

Researchers (Ethier et al., 2004; Mills, 2004; Shaffer, Huston, & Egeland, 2008), made similar findings that the earlier children were abused, the more likely they were to develop behavioral problems in childhood and adolescence. Additionally, these children were shown to internalize feelings of sadness, isolation, and depression, and to be either, withdrawn or aggressive, or both.

Twenty Two

In the middle of my senior year, I tried out for a part with a prestigious performance group called Up with Folks. I got the part, but being seventeen and still underage required Ruben and Momma to sign a release in order for me to go. Rehearsals started soon, but the troupe would not be on the road until early summer, right after I graduated from high school. I begged, and pleaded, to no avail. Convinced that the best place for me was with them, they refused to sign because they didn't think I was mature enough. And that was that. I moved on to the next strategy. Being a flight attendant would be a great job! I could travel the world, make money, and most importantly, leave my chaotic life behind. After high school, I worked, attended community college, and applied for flight attendant jobs. In those days, the company mailed a postcard with information like . . . where interviews were being held, how to get tickets to the destination, what hotel to stay in, how to present yourself, etc. I'd interviewed for TWA several times. Momma called me at work one day to tell me I'd received a postcard. I'd been hired. When I got off work it was so late that everyone had gone to bed. I searched for the card high and low, but couldn't find it. The following morning I asked her. Looking incredibly guilty because she was such a terrible liar, she said she must have been mistaken, that no such card had arrived. I sat looking at her incredulously! I couldn't believe it.

"Then why did you call me at work?"

"It was a mistake," she repeated looking like a child caught with her hand in the cookie jar.

I couldn't believe what I was hearing. I was dumbfounded, blind-sided, and utterly gob-smacked! Why would she sabotage me like that? Why would she do that to me? Without the card, I would miss my meeting.

Aaron took me aside later that day to tell me that she and Ruben sat together discussing what to do next, and the last time he'd seen the card was in Ruben's hand. I felt so powerless, so I quit applying for flight attendant jobs because I couldn't trust that I would receive my mail, and never told them anything about my plans again.

Twenty Three

Over time, the once vibrant neighborhood in which Gram lived was taken over and zoned for business until the only family residence left on the block was hers. Except for her stint in Drumright, Oklahoma with her second abusive husband, she lived in that little house just all her adult life—sleeping on a cot next to the kitchen until her death. During hot, muggy summers, the only cool room in the house was the bedroom she'd shared with my grandfather, Andre. In fact, it was ice cold and eerie, and in that room lived the ghosts of the past. A massive blonde bedroom suite with matching dresser and antique silver-plated mirror overwhelmed the tiny room. On the dresser, a framed portrait of Grandfather, a hand-tinted duo tone of a young Ruben and his brothers, smiling and serious faces captured in black and white photos with yellowing, curled edges, rosary beads—all corroborating artifacts from another lifetime—pieces of a story, the story she wants us to see—everything in its proper place, a place in time that didn't really exist. I spent hours trying to fit all the clues together. At the age of seventy seven, she died on Grandfather's birthday. In a vivid dream, she leans over the bed. I feel her lips brush my forehead. Her body glows so brightly I wonder why it doesn't burn.

"What is it Gram?"

"It's time to say goodbye my love."

I awake to the phone ringing. It's Momma. Gram's gone.

After completing basic training in North Carolina, Aaron makes a stop in Sand Springs to see Gram. He rings the doorbell. No answer. Rings again. No answer. It's rare that she doesn't answer. He drives to Uncle Robert's just a few blocks away to see if she's there. She's not, but Robert reassures that everything is fine. Arriving in Kansas City around midnight, he is given the bad news. Robert found her on the floor trying to crawl to the door to answer the bell.

"Did you hear? I'm responsible. I could have saved her. I was there. I couldn't save you and Momma, at least I could have saved her. All I had to do was break down the door. I could have saved her. I knew something was wrong."

"How could you have known Aaron? It's not your fault. It's no one's fault. She had cancer. She'd been sick a very long time. It's not your fault."

He is inconsolable. Nothing I say helps.

A quick stop at Gram's after the funeral becomes a life-changing event for me. Clothing entrails snake from under beds, and out of closets and drawers. Cabinet doors are flung wide with the contents dumped and strewn everywhere. Her house is in utter disarray. She'd been a very private person in life, and her house was usually neat as a pin with everything in its place.

"Better get yourself some of this shit. If you don't, it'll all be gone," Ruben snaps angrily from the doorway. "If you had played your cards right, she would have left everything she had to you. She really loved you. For what reason, I'll never know."

Aaron blames himself. Ruben blames him. Ruben exacts payback by turning her death into Aaron's failure—my neglect. We are now twenty eight and twenty six, and still the scapegoats, responsible for Gram dying of breast cancer. When he is out of earshot, Anna whispers, "Don't worry," but she does not do this in front of him because there are rules. This one says—No empathy allowed for Aaron or me. I take a nightgown from her top drawer—bury my face in it—and inhale deeply. That's what I take.

We go directly to the family dinner at Uncle Robert's. The table is set with southern foods; casseroles, fried chicken, potato salad, beans and rice, pork chops, fruit, homemade macaroni and cheese, and homemade pies, all brought by Gram's Church members, friends, and family. We sit on the front porch with plates balanced on our laps. Intense, angry yelling breaks the surface tension of the bubble . . . not uncommon at family get-togethers, somber funerals included. I should be used to the mountain of gunpowder exploding, but I have no tolerance for it any more. Unfolding before us is an episode of the 'Jerry Springer Show', and how would it be a good episode without a free-for-all fight scene? In the red corner, we have Rubennnn! And in the blue, his brother Warrennn! Ding, ding, ding, ding. Ruben grabs a handful of Warren's hair while simultaneously landing hard uppercuts to his face and chin. Ohhhh! Not exactly Marcus of Queensbury rules, but effective!

"You were always a cruel son-of-a-bitch, always bullying us! There wasn't a dog or cat for miles around that you didn't kill, or torture! You even killed my cat! You ain't normal man! You don't have feelings like other people," Warren screeches. Oops! Can't let the cat out of the bag! Not here anyway; too many eyes and ears. Robert manages to wedge them apart. Break! Ruben turns away.

Yes, it's over. Nothing more to see folks. No clear winner, just a bunch of losers.

Ruben screams, "You're trying to cheat me out of my share you son-of-a-bitch! I know there's more, you dirty bastard!"

Ohhh, no! Ruben blindsides Warren with a barrage of one-two punches giving him a bloody nose. The ref dives in, calls for another break! Ding, ding, ding, ding. Robert's neighbors have stopped tending barbecues, washing cars, and playing softball. No cheers from the crowd—just crickets and stares. Slowly, one by one, they look away. What's most disturbing is the collective reaction of the family. They go on filling paper plates and Dixie cups with food and drink as if nothing's out of place. Can't prove it, but I surmise that Ruben was the one who tore Gram's little house apart looking for anything of value. How else would he have known the little strong box, the one he beat up Warren over, was gone? When he couldn't find it, what ensued was the so-called leadership of the family (men in their fifties) engaging in a pugilistic display—settling it with fisticuffs in the middle of the street—on the day of their mother's funeral—with family and strangers ringside. Before going back to California, I attempt to have an adult conversation with him.

"You don't know what you're talking about," he snarls. "I hear that fancy assed husband of yours talking. He's got you brainwashed . . . filling your head with fancy ideas!"

Hollingsworth et al. (2007) posits that scapegoating in the course of a family violence dynamic can dull the ability of witnessing siblings to have empathy for the victimized.

Twenty Four

When fifteen, Momma graduated from high school as class Valedictorian . . . only two years after her father's death. Her speech was titled: "Finding your niche." In September, her mother, Bella, unceremoniously packs her bags, telling her she had a scholarship waiting at Tuskegee, and that once she left, not to come back.

"But Mother, I don't have clothes to wear. I don't want to go to college," she protests. "I want to stay here and work."

Before the words are out of her mouth, she is lying on the floor holding her face. "Don't back sass me girl! Do it again and I'll knock your teeth down your throat. You can't stay here! Pack your things! It's time to go! My job is done."

I know this story by heart because Momma told it often. Bella wanted to remarry, and couldn't have the daughters from a previous husband underfoot. By this time, Charisma has married in a shotgun wedding and moved away. Leslie is in nursing school. And now, it's Momma's turn to go.

She turned sixteen a couple of months after arriving on campus, and she was so ill prepared for life. The only places she'd been allowed to go before now were church, home, or school. That was it. In the beginning of her senior year, she met a handsome soldier named Ruben and promptly became pregnant. At least, that's the story they told. I found out that she and Ruben met in Okmulgee, Oklahoma when she was a kid, and he was there visiting his uncle who lived across the street from her family. When they reconnected, she traded the prospects of career (she wanted to be a chemist) for a wedding ring (her niche). Not long after the birth of her first child (that would be me), he receives orders for Stuttgart and finagles blood tests by telling her it's a military requirement. She complies—packs her baby for an arduous bus trip across Base requiring two transfers each way. Once the results are in, he reads them incorrectly and beats the crap out of her. That's when she found out the test was for paternity blood typing, and was not required for their upcoming trip. I also know this story by heart because I grew up on it.

Early in the relationship, he lied, and she believed his lies. He takes over the abusive parent roll; a vacuum left by her mother, and systematically strips Momma of her power, intelligence, feelings, and thoughts. He is contrite only after a doctor reads the results correctly, and she believes the first violent episode to be an isolated anomaly, as do many women enmeshed in abusive relationships. The first honeymoon ensues. He'd met a woman on his first tour of duty in Germany, and they had a son. Ruben actually requested to be stationed in Stuttgart so he could see his son and bring him back to the States. He told Momma of his intentions only after they were in Stuttgart, and only after the ex-girlfriend and his first-born child were sitting in the living room. When presented with this development, Momma refused to believe it, and immediately got pregnant with Aaron. He physically and verbally abused her while she was carrying Aaron as retribution. She wrote her sister for money to escape, but since he controlled everything, the letter containing the money was intercepted. He beat her in retaliation for plotting behind his back. I was two or three when she chose me as confidante. The story was so distressing I never forgot it.

Over the years, she rationalized why she hadn't sent him on down the road kicking rocks after they got back to the States when there were only two children. I'm about eight the first time I ask, "Then why do you keep having so many babies? Why don't you leave him now before it gets worse?"

"Well, we're Catholic."

That explanation made no sense whatsoever at the time. What did religion have to do with it? I'd been in a Catholic church at least once for a funeral. The—"We're Catholic"—answer was yet, another, in a very long line of excuses. It was only after Aaron's death that I seriously considered how her early life molded her responses to negative events.

During the fifties and sixties, people were encouraged to have big families to replenish the war machine, and many of those having large families came from large families in which abuse occurred. Women had no access to birth control and, in fact, were discouraged from its use. Additionally, they were discouraged from divorcing no matter how bad or violent the relationship. No support existed for women—no shelters, no community protection, no protection from the law. So the only thing left to do was cover up and teach your children to cover up. When you are taught to cover up the truth by any means necessary as a trans-generational coping strategy, what is right in front of you is often hardest to see. My mother was trapped. We were trapped and the most difficult trap for me was being required to pretend everything was just fine when it wasn't.

Twenty Five

He harasses me with demeaning, venom filled phone calls. No, he isn't drunk! He's a "roid" raging cokehead. You know the little kit with the needles and vials of clear liquid I found in his closet years earlier? Winstrol was one of the most popular anabolic steroids of the late seventies, early eighties. And for a narcissistic, sociopath in the throes of "roid" rage and a coke habit, I become the reason for all the ills in his world. The more he rages, the more I pull away. I'm scared of him. I don't trust him. I unplug the phone around seven or eight in the evening when the calls are likely to start, and I cut Momma off, too, by staying away. She has no one to confide in. Occasionally, he shows up on my doorstep unannounced. I call the cops to have him escorted away.

With me out of the picture, her buffer zone is gone. The stabilizing leg has been knocked from under the teetering structure of their marriage. It was okay to stay with him as long as Aaron and I took some of the pressure off. So now, the beatings are no longer divided among three of us. I am seething with anger toward them because I am aware of being used and I feel a deep sense of betrayal. The coping skills developed to survive childhood fail me in my new life. I'm angry and suffer from anxiety and severe panic attacks and anorexia. To finish the job they started, I smoke pot to calm down, and pop speed to rev up. Pot and anorexia may seem contradictory since it gives you the munchies, but not when you do speed as well. I got some shady doctor to prescribe Black Beauties for weight loss. One in the morning and I'm good the rest of the day until weighing in at a skeletal, sunken cheeked, eight two pounds. My mind plays tricks on me. In the mirror, I see a blob. I have no control over the panic attacks, but I control what I put in my mouth.

My friend, Amanda notices the extreme weight loss, confides to me about her abusive family, her mental break, and subsequent treatment.

"Remember when we first met in the laundromat? Well, I never told you that it was my Aunt Lacey who saved my life. I tried to commit suicide. It was serious enough for me to be hospitalized. She'd always been my favorite even though we never spent much time around her. My parents talked about her like she was some weirdo, but she wasn't. When she found out I was in the hospital, she drove all the way from Kansas City to Milwaukee to get me and bring me home with her. She took care of me the rest of my senior year in high school. She had a friend who was a psychologist and set up therapy for me with him. If it hadn't been for her, I wouldn't be here now. I wouldn't have made it. You need help. You've got to go."

At first I argue, but she wears me down. A side effect of growing up the way I did is the inability to trust, but for some reason I allow her to guide me to mental health services. She holds my hand and sits in the waiting room to make sure I get the help I so desperately need.

"You'll see. You're not awful," she kept saying. "Don't be afraid. It's going to be all right."

Her honesty was a generosity that probably saved my life. She was an Angel sent to walk across my stage with a perfectly timed message, and that walk-on was ultimately responsible for transforming my belief in the process of therapy. All the years I'd tried to convince Momma to do better had fallen on deaf ears because she wasn't ready to hear the message and maybe she never would be. And whether I thought it was good or bad was insignificant. It was her path to walk, not mine. My parents made me the bad guy because I asked for something they couldn't comprehend. They didn't know how to be different. Amanda was right. I wasn't the bad person they'd made me out to be. I got it on an intellectual level, but my numbed feelings were difficult to deal with, too much at one time, overwhelming.

During one session Dr. Davis asks, "Is your father a drug addict or alcoholic? His behavior is indicative of addiction, among other things."

"Oh, yes."

"Does one of your parents have an eating disorder?"

"Yes, I'm pretty sure my mother does."

I see Dr. Davis for the good part of a year. When I start to feel worthy, I gain weight. I start to feel better about myself until Aaron moves in. Ruben uses Aaron as my Achilles heel and pits us against each other. Where I've been able to keep him at arms length for a year and a half, he's now attempting to weasel in through an open window. I'm torn. I want Aaron in my life, but I don't want the 185-pound gorilla attached to him and there is a real danger of losing the gains I've made, of collapsing under the pressure of school, job, and bills. He uses money to control my mother and siblings and make himself look good in front of others. He promises to pay Aaron's tuition—tells lies, brags about how he pays for his kid's educations to anyone who appears to be listening—strangers, acquaintances, extended family. Aaron wants to believe—has trouble transitioning—gets sucked into the maelstrom. I suggest therapy for him as well. He refuses. We have huge arguments.

"But he gives you money. He told me so. He tells everyone he pays your way."

"That's not true! He's lying as usual! He's manipulating you. He's using you. It was so hard for me to save enough money to move out because he and Momma kept borrowing what little I had. There was always something—school pictures, new shoes, groceries for the family. He was always saying he'd pay me back, but never did. He made it hard for me. They both did. I got smart and started lying about how much money I made. Think about it . . . if he had enough money to send us to college, why did he need to take my money? He hasn't given me shit since I've been here because I don't matter, and neither do you. I work! And I barely make ends meet! That's why you have to work, too! Don't rely on him!"

After three months of expecting money that never comes, Aaron breaks down and finally gets a job. Our start may have been rocky, but we do manage to find happy footing—exploring newfound freedoms—clubbing, the music scene, and, of course, drugs and alcohol. There is no shortage of people with the same interests, no shortage of people our age!

Twenty Six

She got pregnant with their seventh child shortly after I moved out. At four months along she tells me she is finally getting a divorce. By the time her court date rolls around, she is eight months. Since she seemed earnest this time, I showed up as moral support, but mainly I came because I wanted to see it for myself. As though he were admonishing a petulant child, the male judge insultingly asks why she wants the divorce. What's it to him? Does he know, or even care what we've been through? Of course, not! For twenty years of hell, he granted short-term spousal support, a child support pittance that was rarely paid, and nothing more; no furniture; no car; no nothing! She is paralyzed with fear.

"After you have this baby, you need to get a job. Stop depending on him," I urge.

Her flippant comeback is stunning.

"I shouldn't have to work! He owes me!"

Two years later, I receive an emotional phone call. She has two weeks to find an apartment because spousal support has run out, and she needs to find affordable housing. During the late seventies, an African-American woman with more than one child was likely to be denied rental housing in most suburban neighborhoods. Mostly, she's denied because of a lack of credit history. I suspect the number one reason is stereotyping. After filling out an application, the manager waits a day or two before coming back with the no credit history excuse to make it look like they at least tried. The rental agents never look us in the eye.

At the last complex on the list, the manager, a woman, gives us the no credit history excuse, but something about her demeanor is reminiscent of Mrs. Pena, at the Teacher's Credit Union years before. I run with it. My mother and sisters quietly listened to me argue their case for a solid hour in that claustrophobic little office. Finally relenting, the manager admits to her own battles with an abusive husband and a messy divorce the year previous.

Momma's first apartment is a two bedroom for $140.00 a month, and apartment they will later refer to as the "Roach Motel". She counts out the money. I add another $60.00 to the pot and buy groceries for them with my last $20.00. I am flat broke—no money until the next payday. I didn't do it for her. I did it for my sisters. Maybe it was fear, but Momma's non-action seems so incongruous of an adult woman with children to care for. My parting words to her were: "You cannot rely on him. You need to get a job!"

The following week, Aaron pays for the U-Haul and we pitch in to help them move. Aaron lifts couches and boxes with an ace bandage wrapped around his sprained ankle.

With a Bachelor degree, a teaching credential, and classroom experience, she was better off than many women in her position. And, although the country was in the throes of a deep recession, oil embargo, and high unemployment, she managed to snag a minimum wage job at a well-known department store . . . $400 every two weeks to be divided between rent, daycare, food and necessities. With three children at home, it's a tight fit because she cannot count on child support. Alas, there is no happy ending.

Lifelong programming cannot be undone in a few short months, or years, or in Momma's case, ever. From Ruben's standpoint, he owns her and the kids, and back in the day his viewpoint was reinforced by a male concentric judicial system that aided and abetted his campaign of economic vengeance against her. That system protected his right to plausible patriarchal deniability by looking the other way when women like my mother attempted to bring action for child support enforcement. Instead of receiving help, they were sent away with a pat on the head and treated like wayward whores. He makes payments whenever he wants while wining and dining his girlfriends at the best restaurants, buying new cars and purchasing expensive hang-gliders at six to seven thousand dollars a pop. All this while his three children living with Momma languished in abject poverty. The main objective was to squeeze her so hard she would fail and come running back to him. Arianne, Socorro, and Anna contribute to her household from part time jobs. They also do the best they can to rear their youngest sister—cooking, housekeeping, laundry, buying diapers and food, all while attending school. And although, they don't have to watch or experience the weekly beatings, they are hostages of our parent's abusive psychological warfare against each other. Meanwhile, I do my best not to cross paths with him because on the rare occasions I do, he threatens to kill me for breaking up his happy family.

"If you hadn't helped her, your Momma wouldn't have left me. The next time you stick your nose in, I'll beat your little black ass to a bloody pulp and then, break your skinny neck for good measure!"

I take his threats seriously because they are entrenched in the family business of intimidation and control—deeply entrenched in the rhetoric of violence and abuse in which, two sets of rules exist—one for the perpetrator and another for his victims. He threatens Momma with statements like—"If I catch another man around my kids, I'll kill him and then I'll kill you." And he made these threats in front of his children. Then out of the other side of his ass, he bragged about the women he was dating and how he wanted to remarry. But as quickly as those relationships begin, they are over as the latest conquest reels him in, takes a good look at what she's caught, and can't throw him back into the scummy, primordial pond from whence he came fast enough. I am secretly amused.

Twenty Seven

After a year of living on the East coast, Javier and I returned to Lawrence for a month long stopover before continuing on to California. We rent a room from a friend and Javier proceeds to complete his degree work. I'm twenty seven. Momma invites me to spend the night at her new place, and foolishly, I accept the invitation—maybe, because I hadn't seen her for more than a year. She tells me they may be running errands when I arrive—to come on in. She'll leave the backdoor unlocked. Around noon I arrive at her new duplex, which is much nicer than the 'Roach Motel'. Although, she's not working, this time Momma's wrangled Jewel, who works as a flight attendant, into paying the monthly rent. Even with Momma's attitude toward her, Jewel still tries to win her love.

I park myself in a chair and turn on the TV and just as I get comfortable, the door opens. It's him! They've now been divorced for seven years, yet he walks into her house like he owns it. I am sure he has manipulated one of his minions into giving up information about my arrival (probably Socorro, or maybe even Momma), and has been lying in wait all day like an ambush predator. It's been two years since I last saw him, four since I've stepped foot inside his house. That last face-to-face didn't go well. He'd exploded and threatened to kill me. I got the hell out of there. Everyone kept trying to get me to come back. They said I was just being paranoid . . . that he really wouldn't hurt me . . . and that he doesn't mean the things he says or does. They try to make it sound like I'm just making trouble, and that I don't have any reason to avoid him.

Telling the truth about our parents is considered treason. I call Bullshit! All I have to do is think about is how he killed Ruffo, and put him in the garbage for me to find. And let's not forget he's threatened to do the same to me more than once. Exhibiting the antecedent behaviors, the wind up to violence . . . the screeching, wild gesturing, and crazy eyes, he starts in.

"You ungrateful little bitch! How come you didn't call me when you got back in town? Who the hell do you think you are?" I spring from the chair, and run out the front door to my car. When certain he's not following, I pull to the shoulder of the road and experience a severe panic attack . . . wave after wave of nausea, crying, shaking, racing heart, sweating.

Javier meets me at the door. He's my protector. He's worried.

"You look terrible. Your mom's been calling. What happened?"

He listens patiently as I relate my story.

"He's dangerous. He's really, really dangerous! I know you want to see your mom and sisters, but it's not safe for you there! They're not going to look out for you."

The ringing phone interrupts our conversation. It's her.

"I had a feeling it was something like that because when I got back he was yelling at everyone. Well, he's just mad because you keep avoiding him. He's still your father, you know. When you were little, he thought you were the cutest little thing."

"Oh, stop making excuses for him! I wasn't even two before he started hitting me in the mouth."

"I don't remember that," she refutes even though she's admitted to it in the past.

Her memory is selective and dependent on whether or not she has a bone to pick with him.

"Well, I do and I don't give a damn who he is, or what's best for him. Why do you want me to sit at the table with my abuser and pretend everything is copacetic? Why do you keep sticking up for him? Why do you continue to let that madman hijack your family? No matter how much you try, you will never convince me he's this wonderful, somewhat misguided, misunderstood person! I know better! It seems to me you've got a decision to make!"

"What's that?" she asks warily.

"It's either me or him!"

I wait for her to say something, anything . . . can feel her struggling. Finally, and with no conviction, she answers, "He's still your father, you know."

I hang up, and we don't speak again for six months.

Twenty Eight

A distraught Aaron knocks on my door one morning saying he needed to talk to me. He'd just been to Kansas City because he was supposed to help Ruben do some yard work. When he got there, he found his girlfriend Laila hiding in a guest bedroom. Devastated—crying and completely beside himself, he was certain Ruben had slept with her. I was inclined to believe him given the circumstances and Ruben's track record with women. Our father was so jealous of Aaron that he would have done anything to demean him, including sleeping with his girlfriend. That incident spurred Aaron to take stock of his life. Up to that point, he'd knocked around from one menial job to another, so enlisting in the military seemed like a good idea.

At twenty five, he was older than the average recruit, but he'd made up his mind to be a better person, to make a better life for himself. I thought he was still trying to win Ruben's love and respect, something that was never going to happen. Ruben never had anything positive to say about his only son—called him lazy, told him he'd never amount to nothin', told him he was worthless. In reality, Aaron was industrious and resourceful—always had a job, whether loading and unloading trucks, stocking grocery shelves, bussing dishes, or his real love, working on cars and motorcycles. He was sensitive, intelligent, artistic and creative, and loved tinkering with what most people considered junk. From that junk emerged little mechanical creations.

"This stupid shit ain't going to make any money. You're just wasting your time. Anybody can make this crap better than you, including me! Get your goddamned head out of the clouds boy," Ruben berated.

While Jewel, Aaron, and I suffered symptoms of PTSD in varying combinations, each of us dealt with the abuse in very different ways. I walked away seething with a deep, smoldering rage and resentment for both our parents. Jewel continued to try to help Momma in an attempt to gain her love until finally realizing that no matter what she did her mother would never love her. Eventually, she walked away, hardened by that fact. Aaron limped away using artful camouflage to disguise the hole in his soul, he wrestled with feelings of inadequacy and worthlessness all of his life.

After Basic he was stationed in Stuttgart—in the place he was born—full circle. His letters are filled with Reggae driven escapades of London nightlife, the music scene, and coming into his own. He seemed happy. After returning to the States I see him on one of my short visits to Momma's.

"Do you think you want to make the military your life?" I ask.

"When you sign on the dotted line, they own your ass. Sometimes I feel trapped like when we were at home. No, it's not what I want to for the rest of my life."

Reluctantly re-upping after three months of not being able to find a job. His next orders were for Seoul, Korea. Two years later, he was diagnosed with paranoid schizophrenia, bipolar disorder, and PTSD by military doctors, and received an Honorable Discharge. After that, everything about him was different. I wasn't sure I could believe a long rambling story he told.

"I was the leader of a drug ring that delivered crank to villages on the outskirts of Seoul. Only Koreans rode the trains that far from base, but when I started seeing more Americans, I got paranoid CID was following me. My commander wanted me to take a drug test, so I stayed up all night drinking water to dilute my pee. The next thing I remember is waking up in a VA hospital back in the States."

Here's what I made of it. He told me he was thinking about going into Special Forces, just like Ruben. The pressure caused him to suffer a severe mental break. And there were any number of things that could have triggered it ... loneliness, a combination of loneliness and pressure ... untreated PTSD from childhood ... not having dealt with Gram's death ... drug use ... our family's genetic propensity for mental illness ... and or, all of the above. No matter how you look at it, the combination was a recipe for disaster. And I'm skeptical of the schizophrenia diagnosis because the military's track record for providing even negligible psychiatric services in the 1980's was pretty much non-existent. I believe he wasn't given a Medical discharge so the government could avoid paying him a disability pension.

Soon after being discharged, he met a woman named Katie during a lucid period and moved to Florida for a few years. In 2000, he was back in Dallas. That was the last time I saw him alive. In 2003, Momma asked him to leave her house because she became fearful during one of his acute episodes of psychosis. He'd become violent and had accused her elderly neighbors of spying on him, poisoning the water, etc. But I also believe that the pressure of being around the family was too much. As he broke down, Momma called to ask Javier what to do.

He said, "Call the police. Tell them he needs a 72-hour involuntary psychiatric commitment, and make sure they know he doesn't have any weapons."

In 2004, Aaron committed himself to the VA hospital in Oklahoma and moved to Los Angeles shortly after being released. We kept in touch sporadically as he cycled through good and bad years. 2005 and 2006 were good years. In 2006, when Omar was nine, Javier planned a visit to his parent's home in southern California. I couldn't be there because of a business trip, but I asked Aaron to meet them so he could meet his nephew for the first time. The last photos any of us have of him were taken then. In one, he stands next to Omar, and in the other he sits atop his prized Harley. He looks physically well, but the sparkle is gone from his eyes.

I flew to LA three months later for a visit we'd planned over several months, but he wouldn't see me, nor would he let me know where he lived, nor could I coax him out.

"I'm sorry it didn't work out this time Leanne. Maybe, next time," he apologized.

"It's okay, Aaron, I understand. I'll see you next time."

To be honest, I was heartbroken. I didn't want to understand, but if I applied too much pressure, he'd disappear. Fighting back tears, I tell him how much I love him. After hanging up, I have a vivid premonition. He was saying goodbye, and this had been my last opportunity to see him alive.

September 2007, he calls to tell me he's getting married in October—gives me his new number.

"Leanne, stay in contact with James. He really wants to know my family. No one else in the family accepts him, but I know you do."

"I will," I promise.

"I love you. You were always my favorite sister."

"I love you too. You are my favorite brother."

We laugh.

"I'd love to meet your new fiancé and spend some time with you, if that's okay."

He says, "Okay," and that turns out to be the last real conversation we have—too much pressure. He disappeared again.

I know the hang-ups are from him. I needed to pick up after two rings or he'd hang up. It's like having one of those psychic dreams where you answer the ringing phone, but the message is all garbled and you can't shake the feeling you've missed the most important call of your life. He believed the FBI was watching him—watching us—that they could hear his every thought—that they knew when he used the phone—could locate him—and if he lingered too long, they'd come to take him away. On the occasion I answered before he hung up, I'd have to make it quick.

"Hello. How are you? I'm glad you called. I love you. Was that you calling the last few days?"

"Yeah, I thought your phone might be tapped."

His answers were affirmations of the incredible pain, paranoia, and confusion he suffered.

In late May 2008, I was getting those hang-up calls. I work at home, so I'm usually pretty close to the phone.

After taking a short break, the voicemail light is flashing. It's an automated message from the Sonoma County North Detention Center asking if I will accept a collect call from an inmate? The inmate's name is Aaron. Yolanda searches the rosters for his name. I'm praying, hoping, thinking he's made his way to Santa Rosa somehow.

"I can't find him. I'm sorry," she replies. My voice cracks. "I'm desperate to find him. Can you tell me anything else? I know it's him."

"Does he have mental problems, honey?" she asks.

"Yes."

She volunteers her story of growing up in violence and how mental illness has affected her family, and that's why she's rearing her niece and nephew. Her sister is severely bi-polar. We are both crying by the time she finishes.

"It's funny how you wish they were in jail so at least you know where they are," I say.

"Yes, I feel the same way. Maybe he'll call tomorrow. If he does, it'll probably be around the same time. I'll pray for you."

"I'll pray for you as well."

We say our goodbyes.

I don't know what I can do for him. I don't want to invite him to live in my home with my son . . . too unpredictable . . . too chaotic and I don't do chaos anymore. I also don't want Omar to live in a household with someone who suffers from psychosis, could be violent, and doesn't take his meds. He deserves what Aaron and I didn't have—a stable, non-violent home. Not in a million years, did I ever think I'd have to choose between my beloved brother and my son. I decide to try to get him some services! I wait for a call that never comes.

I found out that the call came from the North County Detention Center because calls from the system are routed through the closest facility. He was calling Los Angeles. The phone number he always called me on was the only listed number we had. I hadn't needed that particular number for five years, but kept it just so he could get in touch with me. He died in August and I reluctantly cancelled the service in October.

A number of studies indicate that histories of childhood maltreatment have been observed in a large percentage of adults with severe and persistent mental illness. A significant connection was also found between childhood stressors such as physical abuse and neglect and how symptoms of adult onset schizophrenia manifest (Gallagher III & Jones; 2013). Researchers discovered that the type of childhood stressor such as physical abuse or neglect often predicted whether specific symptoms of adult onset schizophrenia were aggression or withdrawal. Physical abuse incubated aggression and neglect withdrawal.

Twenty Nine

Aaron's death leaves me emotional and angry. I finally do what my therapists have urged all along; I confront him. The first thing out of his mouth is: "I wish I'd never had any of you kids. Heh! Heh! Heh!" The heh—heh—heh's are supposed to be a thinly disguised mask for anger.

"Is this really what you want to say after all these years? So, why did you?"

"Why did I what?"

"Why did you have us?"

"Well, your Momma, she kept getting pregnant. What was I supposed to do? I had a son with my German girlfriend before she came along and tricked me into marrying her black nappy ass. She ruined everything. I didn't want to marry her!"

"You do know how babies are made, don't you?" I ask sarcastically.

"You're bringing this shit up? The last time I spoke to your brother he was talking the same crap!"

"What did you tell him?"

"I told him to stay in the Army. They couldn't just put him out like that! Neither of you ever listened to me!"

"So, let me get this straight. You're blaming him for being sick?"

"Why are you bringing this shit up? It's over, in the past. You need to let bygones be bygones, and just go along with the program."

"What program?"

"You know what program!"

"I'm a little fuzzy. Why don't you explain it to me?"

"My house, my rules—I could do what I wanted. You and your brother were always interfering—always trying to protect her! It was none of your goddamned business! We'd still be together, if it hadn't been for you!"

"But you said she trapped you! Why didn't you just leave?"

"Is that why you haven't spoken to me in twenty years? You didn't even have the common courtesy to tell me I had another grandson. I had to hear about it from other people. You did it to embarrass me!"

"Oh please! Don't flatter yourself! After I had my son, you were the last person on my mind. You never gave a damn about me!"

"You know I love you sugar pie? Don't you?"

"I see you for what you really are. I'm not looking at who I wish you were."

"How can you say that?" he asks in a whiny high-pitched voice. "What do you know about anything?"

"I know I've never hit, beaten, or demeaned my son. I don't blame him for my problems. He can have friends over without worrying about whether his father will beat up his mother in front of them. His father has never threatened to kill him. He's not afraid of either of his parents. We take care of him, not the other way around. He gets to be himself. He is not my confidante, sounding board, or whipping boy. And most of all, we like and love him with our hearts. That's what I know."

"I'm old and dying. I have grandparent's rights! If I took it to court, they'd order you to let me see my grandson cause you don't know your head from a hole in the ground!"

"I don't know my head from a hole in the ground? What makes you think the courts will take the word of a convicted batterer and sociopath over mine? If you want to spend your last days fighting it, then by all means go for it. All I have to do is bring up how you beat up your girlfriend and then pulled a gun on her. I know exactly how it went down because I've seen and heard it all before. I lived it. But in 2000, the changing tide of the justice system caught up with you. The DA prosecuted you because what you did is considered a crime. And what you did to us back then is also a crime. You took a plea to keep from going to jail, and were ordered to pay $17,000 in restitution and given four years probation, but as far as I'm concerned you got off easy. They should have locked your ass up and thrown away the key! Grandparent's rights my ass," I end derisively.

Silence, nothing but silence. I wait for a volley. He clears his throat. I wait. Dried twigs snapping, "Well I guess you're not like your Momma, are you?" he croaks.

"Who ever said I should be?"

"Then what about forgiveness?"

"If you didn't do anything wrong, why would you need forgiveness? Besides, if you really wanted to work it out with me, you could have called. I've had the same number for thirty years!

"You don't understand. I had to have some way of keeping you all in line. If I kept you in line, the others would follow. How could I have known your brother was a goddamned mental case?"

"How could you have known? There were signs. It runs in our family. What about the time your aunt threw her husband's little dog out of a moving car right in front of us? Uncle Warren's son blew his brains out. Was that just an anomaly, some incident that happened in a vacuum? Uncle Robert's son has been in and out of mental institutions since he was fourteen. Everyone said Aunt Ella was crazy as a "betsy" bug. I'm sure your father beat you and your mother. You beat Aaron and me, killed my dog, and then told me how to feel about it. Why am I supposed to continue protecting your reality?

Let me put it to you this way. When you were in the military, if you saw the enemy burying landmines, would you walk over them? Of course not! Why do you expect me to walk over the ones you've buried and take my little boy with me?"

I wait for him to catch up. Nothing. Finally, in a barely audible whisper, like the wind's been knocked out of him—"You don't know what you're talking about."

Thirty

I reread the CHP report. No more phone calls out of the blue. He isn't going to magically get better. He's really gone. I had a brother one day, and the next all that's left are memories and old photographs. The pain is most acute when I lie down at night and stop running. I cry myself to sleep almost every night. Getting back to the living is slow and painful—grief therapy every Wednesday, sleepless nights, nightmares, panic attacks, unpleasant memories, PTSD. I feel guilty for being the one who survived. I took care of him when we were kids. I feel regret at not having done more. On a head level I know I'm not responsible, but on a heart level, the guilt and pain is almost unbearable. Grief therapy helps me accept that I am not responsible, that I should not feel guilty because he would not have wanted that for me. Time passes. Losing him still feels almost as raw as the day I got that phone call. Two dates arrive within weeks of each other—August 16th, the day he died, and September 3rd, the day he was born. On what should have been his 51st birthday I write a message on a balloon, say a prayer, and watch it ascend and finally disappear into the heavens on invisible breezes. The message: "I love you Aaron. I will miss you till we meet again." He slipped out the back door like when we lived in the desert and I am reminded of him in fleeting glances . . . in a man walking across the street . . . Omar's eyes . . . a cloud shaped like a man riding a Harley . . . the voice of a stranger . . . and the homeless men and women I see every day. They, like my brother have hidden histories of pain, stories we see, but choose not to acknowledge, and rarely do we hear them.

Aaron talked about why he wasn't a regular part of his son's life.

"I don't have anything to offer him but misery and grief. I'm not strong enough to break the cycle. I can't do to him what Ruben did to us. It changed me piece by piece, little by little until everything was so out of focus I couldn't see where I fit in the picture."

Just before Christmas in 2009, Momma calls. I'm kind of shocked because she doesn't initiate contact.

"I've been thinking a lot lately," she starts.

"Sounds serious."

She hesitates and that hesitation makes me nervous.

"I know why you stayed away all this time. But I kept hoping you'd see the light. It wasn't you who needed to see it. It was me. I burdened you with my problems and never thought about how it might affect you. That wasn't right. I can't imagine what it must have been like for you and Aaron. Your brother was such a sweet, vulnerable soul. Not you though. You had grit. You had this way of looking right through people, and you caught us in our lies. I should have protected you. I should have left your father and not let it go on. I should have made different choices. You just don't let people abuse your children like that," she blurts in a rush of words.

She stops abruptly, takes a short pause. In my mind's eye, she is staring into space with regretful thoughts wrinkling her forehead, taking a long sip of over sweetened coffee, followed by a deep drag off her cigarette.

"Do you remember the day you moved to Lawrence?"

"Yes."

"I kept thinking about how you were leaving me behind, and how you had no right. I was petrified of being alone with him. I needed you but, until that moment, I never thought about how you might have needed me."

"What I remember most is you hugged me for the first time. I didn't know how to act, so I tensed up."

"I know. I wanted you all to hurry up and grow up, but that moment came all too quickly," she finishes in a melancholy whisper.

Although her prison didn't involve steel bars, the legal system, and a jury of one's own peers, I can't remember a time when my mother was not a prisoner. She went from an abusive mother, the only prison not of her choosing—to an abusive husband—and then to self-imposed lock down with her adult children as the jailers. She had no friends outside of us—no dinner, movies, drinks, and giggles with the girls—not one date after divorcing Ruben—just day in, day out captivity. After retiring, she spent the last twelve years of her life sitting in front of the TV watching Nancy Grace and Investigation Discovery, drinking coffee and smoking cigarettes, biding her time, blaming retirement for her declining health, complaining about the curse of growing old—waiting for her children, or grandchildren to call or stop by—waiting for life to happen, or death to end it. Always waiting.

Momma never broke the chains of her personal prison. She was too fearful to do anything differently, choosing instead to give up her life to the preternatural forces of the Bible, Jesus, Satan, God, sacrifice, and penitence like a good little martyred Church Lady should. Her tortured mind teetered in depression and tottered within the subtleties of denial and delusion in a cycle of helplessness. And even though her eyes were open, and her body walked the Earth until May of 2013, Momma had long been dead. Try as I may to remember a time when she was truly present, I couldn't. A weight was lifted off my shoulders, and it was the first time I realized there was nothing I could have done to stop it. There was nothing I could have done to save Aaron. The train that carried us here left the station generations ago.

That day, I realized forgiveness does not mean closing my eyes to reality. Forgiveness does not mean allowing myself to be sucked into codependency. But that day, I saw her humanity and forgave the little girl whose growth and development was halted by many traumas, the little girl who never had an opportunity to grow up, and the little girl who stunted her growth by marrying the familiar. What a terrible way to live. How horrible it must have been for her—how helpless and powerless she must have felt. For the first time in a long, long time, I wanted to hug the fragile, shattered human being my mother had become. I had to let it go. It was time to let it go. She did what she thought was best at the time.

The view is spectacular from my back yard deck . . . rolling hills sparsely covered in gnarly native oak and Manzanita. The day is bright with sunshine, bird song, and Sonoma County's warm Mediterranean climate. I drink in the beauty and serenity while mulling over Momma's words. How difficult it must have been for her to admit those things. Cottony clouds hang weightlessly in an azure sky. A large eagle glides lazily into view from the east.

Red-tailed hawks are common. Seeing an eagle is a rare treat. It lazily loops in ever widening circles until directly overhead. I am mesmerized. A soft breeze brushes my upturned face. Elation and joy overwhelms me. Fine dust particles, little pinpoints of light rain down, enveloping me in love. I feel him everywhere and I am swept into the giddiness we shared as children. I can smell him, feel his touch, and hear his laughter.

"I love you. I love you. I miss you, Aaron. I love you," I call to the eagle.

Lingering . . . lingering . . . flapping . . . flapping . . . circling . . . circling . . . whoosh . . . whoosh . . . one moment longer . . . slowly, almost reluctantly, it ascends. I watch until it is a speck.

In my dreams that night, he is well and strong. We talk and hang out like old times.

"Did you get my message?" he asks.

"Yes. I knew it was you. I wish you could stay."

He pulls a scroll of glowing paper from his right pocket and unfurls it. Elegant black letters swim into place.

"Stop worrying about me Leanne. It's harder for you than it is for me."

Pointing to each item on the list, he explains what they mean in a familiar language that I've forgotten how to speak.

"Do this for me," he finishes.

"What is it Aaron? I don't understand."

"Yes you do. It will come to you."

He re-rolls the scroll, presses it into my left hand and lovingly pushes my fingers around it. When I wake, the pillow is wet beneath my cheek. I can still feel his touch on my hand.

Ruben dies in 2012 at the age of eighty four. Jewel took care of him in his last days because no one else would. Even though she is seven years younger, and because they are so strangely connected, I predict that Momma will soon follow him to the grave. And she does. Just shy of one year later, she dies of severe hypertension and congestive heart failure while sitting in her chair.

The death of our parents signaled the end of an era for Jewel and I. After many years, we reconnected—at first talking maybe once a month—then once a week. And when we put our two stories together we were able to grasp a more complete picture of our family's sickness. When finally face-to-face for the first time in more than thirty years, time fell away. We are discovering how to be the sisters we should have been all along. If you find something you've always longed for, always dreamed of, always hoped for, always wished for, you do not take it for granted. You cherish it. Nowadays, we talk daily—sometimes about regrets at having missed so much of each other's lives—but we are equally amazed at having found each other wandering in the vast emotional desert of a shattered childhood. We are grateful to have found in each other a kindred soul, a kindred soul who needs no introduction, no explanation. Maybe, time had to pass before we could appreciate each other. Maybe, we had to break the cycle of shame and abuse. Maybe, we had to admit that it all really happened. Maybe, we had to learn how to trust. Maybe time had to pass before we could begin to heal. And maybe, we had to admit that we found a way out of the desert, and that the journey has not been in vain.

Not yet the end

If you, or someone you know is being abused, dial 911, or call the National Domestic Abuse Hotline. 1-800-799-SAFE (7233)

For more information about Mental Illness, contact the National Alliance on Mental Illness – NAMI.

References

Abueg, F.R. & Fairbank, J.A. (1992). Behavioral treatment of posttraumatic stress disorder and co-occurring substance abuse. In P.A. Saigh (Ed.), Posttraumatic stress disorder: A behavioral approach to assessment and treatment (pp.111-146). Needham Heights, MA: Allyn & Bacon.

Afifi, T., Boman, J., Fleisher, W., & Sareen, J. (2009). The relationship between child abuse, parental divorce, and lifetime mental disorders and suicidality in a nationally representative adult sample. *Child Abuse & Neglect, 33*, 139–147.

Dube, S., Anda, R., Felitti, V., Chapman, D., Williamson, D., & Giles, W. (2001). Childhood abuse, household dysfunction, and the risk of suicide throughout the life span: findings from the adverse childhood experiences study. *JAMA, 286(24),* 3089-3096, 3120-3126.

Ethier, L., Lemelin, J. P., & Lacharite, C. (2004). A longitudinal study of the effects of chronic maltreatment on children's behavioral and emotional problems. *Child Abuse & Neglect, 28,* 1265–1278.

Gallagher, B., & Jones, B. (2013). Childhood stressors and symptoms of schizophrenia. Clinical Schizophrenia & Related Psychoses, Fall 2013.

Herman, D.B., Susser, E. S., Struening, E. L., & Link, B. L. (1997). Adverse childhood experiences: are they risk factors for adult homelessness? *American Journal of Public Health. 1997 February; 87*(2): 249–255.

Hollingsworth, J., Glass, J., & Heisler, K. W. (2007). Empathy Deficits in Siblings of Severely Scapegoated Children: A Conceptual Model. *Journal Of Emotional Abuse, 7*(4), 69-88. doi:10.1300/J135v7n04_04.

Kilpatrick, K., Williams, L. M., (1998). Potential mediators of post-traumatic stress disorder witnesses to domestic violence. *Child Abuse & Neglect, 22,* 319-333.

Lamont, A. (2010). *Effects of child abuse and neglect for adult survivors.* National Child Protection Clearinghouse at the Australian Institute of Family Studies. Retrieved 10 December 2012, from <http://www.aifs.gov.au>

McGee, C. (2000). *Childhood Experiences of Domestic Violence*. London: Jessica Kingsley Publishers.

McQueen, D., Itzin, C., Kennedy, R., Sinason, V., & Maxted, F. (2009). *Psychoanalytic psychotherapy after child absue. The treatment of adults and children who have experienced sexual abuse, violence, and neglect in childhood*. London: Karnac Books Ltd.

Mills, C. (2004). *Problems at home, problems at school: The effects of maltreatment in the home on children's functioning at school. An overview of recent research.* London: National Society for the Prevention of Cruelty to Children. Retrieved 5 November 2012, from <https://www.nspcc.org.uk/Inform/publications/Downloads/ problemsathome_wdf48202.pdf>.

Shaffer, A., Huston, L., & Egeland, B. (2008). Identification of child maltreatment using prospective and self-report methodologies: A comparison of maltreatment incidence and relation to later psychopathology. *Child Abuse & Neglect, 32,* 682–692.

Thornton, V. (2014). Understanding the emotional impact of domestic violence on young children. *Educational & Child Psychology, 31,* 90-100.

Yount, K., Li, L. (2009). Women's justification of domestic violence in Egypt. *Journal of Marriage and Family, v17 n5,* 1125-1140.

Made in United States
Orlando, FL
25 April 2022